IDEOLOGY

IDEOLOGY

MIKE CORMACK

Series Editor: John Izod, Department of Film and
Media Studies, University of Stirling

B. T. Batsford Ltd·London

© Michael Cormack 1992

First published 1992

Typeset by Servis Filmsetting Ltd, Manchester
and printed in Great Britain by
BPCC Hazells Ltd
Member of BPCC Ltd

Published by B T Batsford Ltd
4 Fitzhardinge Street, London W1H 0AH

A CIP catalogue record for this book is available from the British Library

ISBN 0 7134 6510 7

CONTENTS

Acknowledgements

Thanks are due to John Izod for his useful comments. Also to Chris
for her help and encouragement – and for keeping me sane as the
deadline approached.

PREFACE

This book has been written with a specific purpose in mind. It is designed to introduce the concept of ideology to students of culture and the media. As such, the examples have been chosen to illustrate different approaches to ideological analysis in these fields. It is not meant to be a full account of ideology. Its aim is to enable students to *use* the concept themselves in their own analytic work. In order to do this most effectively, the book has been structured to allow different uses. It can be worked through progressively from the introductory theoretical sections (chapters 1 to 3) to the examples of analysis in the remaining chapters (arranged in order of increasing complexity, with the final two chapters looking at particularly complex texts). However, it can also be used in other ways – most obviously the analyses can be used without a full study of the opening theoretical chapters. Chapter 2 contains a further development of theoretical issues raised in the first chapter and may be left until after some of the earlier analytical chapters have been studied. Finally, the annotated bibliography should guide readers to other books in this field.

The topics for the analytical chapters have been chosen partly to avoid those which have been discussed elsewhere, and partly to represent cultural products which involve particular complexities. They are not meant to give, in any sense, an overall picture of cultural activity. Nor are they limited to either popular culture or élite culture. For an introductory book on ideology, such limitations would be inappropriate. The hope is that the student will be enabled by the examples to study how ideology works in his or her own context.

Defining ideology

Our first problem concerns the definition of ideology. As the following four quotations make clear, there is no shortage of competing accounts.

1. The theory of ideology states that the ideas and beliefs people have are systematically related to their actual and material conditions of existence (Janet Wolff).[1]
2. Ideology is how the existing ensemble of social relations represents itself to individuals; it is the image a society gives of itself in order to perpetuate itself (Bill Nichols).[2]
3. Ideology . . . is a term used to describe the social production of meanings (John Fiske).[3]
4. Ideology has the function (which defines it) of 'constituting' concrete individuals as subjects (Louis Althusser).[4]

Such a variety of available definitions can be bewildering. The links between beliefs, a society's self-image, the production of meaning and the creation of individual identity may not be immediately apparent. Part of the problem lies in the complexity of the phenomena being analysed. Ideology is concerned with how we as individuals understand the world in which we live. This understanding involves the complexities both of individual psychologies and of social structures. Mediating between these (and overlapping with both) lies the realm of communication (involving language, gesture and imagery, as well as the technological processes of the mass media).

But this is only part of the problem. The other complicating factor is that ideology is, as David McLellan has pointed out, an 'essentially contested concept', that is, one over which there is fundamental disagreement as to its precise meaning and use.[5] This is most clearly seen by looking at the history of the word. It first appears in post-revolutionary France at the end of the eighteenth century, meaning a science of ideas, although, as Jorge Larrain has noted, it is related to earlier concepts in the work of philosophers such as Niccolo Machiavelli (1469–1527), Francis Bacon (1561–1626) and Thomas Hobbes (1588–1679).[6] During the nineteenth century Karl Marx and Friedrich Engels incorporated the concept of ideology into the developing theory of Marxism, removing the term from its French philosophical origins. The classic source for this is their early work, *The German Ideology*, written in the mid-1840s but not published until a Russian translation appeared in 1924.[7] Marx and Engels move away from the original meaning of a mental science towards a definition which emphasizes the distortion which ideology works on beliefs and ideas, using the comparison with a *camera obscura* (an artist's aid, originating in mediaeval times, which reproduces an inverted form of a scene, enabling the artist to make a precise copy). Just as the *camera obscura* distorts its image by inversion, so ideology distorts our ideas about society by inverting (and thus concealing) the relationships of the social structure. For Marx and Engels, this distortion is caused by the mode of production, that is, the economic structure. The way we think is a result of the material situation in which we find ourselves.

> Conceiving, thinking, the mental intercourse of men, appear at this stage as the direct efflux of their material behaviour.[8]

Just as the material situation is dominated by one class, so is the way of thinking in a society.

> The ideas of the ruling class are in every epoch the ruling ideas, i.e. the class which is the ruling *material* force of society, is at the same time its ruling *intellectual* force.[9]

As Terry Lovell has put it, 'Ideology, then, may be defined as the production and dissemination of erroneous beliefs whose inadequacies are socially motivated'.[10] Since, in this view, social structures are dependent on economic structures, the term 'socially motivated' relates ideology to economics.

Althusser

If the debate on ideology effectively begins with Marx and Engels, its more recent development has stemmed from the work of the French philosopher Louis Althusser (1918–1990), particularly his 1970 essay 'Ideology and Ideological State Apparatuses', although the earlier essay 'Marxism and Humanism' (1965) is also important.[11] Althusser develops a theory of ideology which is more concerned with structure than with belief. Influenced by the structural anthropology of Claude Lévi-Strauss and post-Freudian developments in psychoanalysis, his writing is not always easy to follow, but as an introduction two points are worth noting. He emphasizes the 'material existence' of ideology. This refers to ideology's embodiment in the structures and institutions of society, a significant departure from the traditional view of ideology as beliefs and ideas. The institutions of broadcasting, for example, such as the British Broadcasting Corporation, or the Federal Communications Commission in the United States, are as much an embodiment of ideology as the programme material which is broadcast. Similarly the social institution of the family is as much a manifestation of ideology as are the beliefs which people have about it.

A second point to note in Althusser's work is the concern with how we, as individuals, are constituted by ideology. Our sense of ourselves and our role in society are, for Althusser, ideological constructions, maintained by the ever-present working of ideology. He uses the term 'subjectivity' to describe the seeming mental coherence of an individual, intentionally playing on the word's ambiguity between the idea of a *subject of* an action (the person who does the action) and the idea of being *subject to* something else (such as being subject to the law).

> In the ordinary use of the term, subject in fact means: 1. a free subjectivity, a centre of initiatives, author of and responsible for its actions; 2. a subjected being, who submits to a higher authority, and is therefore stripped of all freedom except that of freely accepting his [*sic*] submission.[12]

Although these two points concerning the material existence of ideology and subjectivity will be useful to remember, less useful is Althusser's notion of the Ideological State Apparatus (ISA). He contrasts this with the notion of the Repressive State Apparatus (RSA). The latter refers to the state's means of exercising overt force over its subjects by, for example, using the police, the military and the penal system. The ISA, on the other hand, is the state's means of exercising covert force. It is the means by which ideological dominance is maintained and is seen most clearly in the institutions of religion, education, the parliamentary system, and the mass media. It may seem puzzling that Althusser should wish to identify these as elements of the *state* apparatus. The reason is that the state is identified as the apparatus of the dominant class and therefore the dominant ideology (which the ISA works to reproduce) is the ideology of the state. Thus a broad definition of the state according to its function allows Althusser to see any reproduction of the dominant interest as working for the state. However, this definition tends to conceal real variations, as does the term ISA, with its implication of a monolithic ideological structure enveloping ideological subjects.

Althusser's account of ideology clearly makes it an immensely powerful phenomenon, and one which is necessary for any social life to take place at all.

> Ideology is not an aberration or a contingent excrescence of History: it is a structure essential to the historical life of societies.[13]

The importance he gave to it has been echoed by other writers, even though many have used his work as a source to criticize rather than as a path to follow. In particular, his view of ideology as a massively determining force against which individuals have little power to

react, has come to be seen as both historically inaccurate and theor-
etically naïve.

The articulated definition

It would seem, then, that the variety of definitions can be explained
by the complexity of ideology, the history of the term, and the
contested nature of the concept. However, we are still left with the
problem of formulating a workable account of our own. Rather
than deciding on one or other of the above definitions, a broader but
ultimately more precise view can be outlined by noting how they are
complementary rather than contradictory. That is, they can be articulated (or joined) together to form one complex definition. Rather
than being rival accounts, they can then be seen as referring to
different stages in the same process.

Any society will be organized around a preferred self-image. By
'self-image' is meant the way in which the society is described by its
dominant groups. It is this self-image which unites it, making it
identifiable as a unity. A society undergoing crisis, particularly a
crisis over which groups should be dominant, will manifest competing self-images, but one must eventually become accepted as the
dominant image or else the society will lose its coherence. (Northern
Ireland is an obvious Western European example of a country in
which a conflict between two competing self-images has disrupted
the social fabric). These self-images will form the core of a framework of interlocking concepts (such as democracy, liberty, morality,
justice, race, gender, religion, nationality, etc.). These concepts take
their place in linguistic and social practices which provide the means
by which any member of that society can produce meaning and
thereby communicate with other members of the society. The language is spoken in a particular social context. The interaction
between the symbolic system (spoken language) and the social
system (the framework in which speech takes place) produces meaning. The conceptual framework and its related thesaurus of values
mark the limits of acceptable debate. Language users can use language in new ways but if they move outside the ideological framework they are likely to lose their audience.

The relationship between this framework and the specific mental
contents (such as ideas, representations, beliefs, opinions, values,
and judgments) which derive from it, should be apparent. And if we
consider how we define ourselves ('I am such-and-such a kind of
person') then the link with subjectivity should also become clear.
Each person's self-image is not derived from a value-free, objective
essence of selfhood, a centre of will and intentional action. Rather,

our self-image is socially-derived (language is, after all, a social phenomenon) and is dependent on heavily loaded ideological concepts. We can only define ourselves in social terms.

Ideology, then, is a process which links socio-economic reality to individual consciousness. It establishes a conceptual framework, which results in specific uses of mental concepts, and gives rise to our ideas of ourselves. In other words, the structure of our thinking about the social world, about ourselves and about our role within that world, is related by ideology ultimately to socio-economic conditions. Adding to this Althusser's insistence on the material existence of ideology in social institutions, we get a more comprehensive articulated account than the brief definitions at the beginning of the chapter.

Before continuing, it is worth mentioning the link between this concept of ideology and the common use of the word in everyday political discussion. This latter sense is used to refer to any set of consciously held political beliefs, sometimes with the connotation of dogmatic extremism ('the ideology of fascism', 'the ideology of revolutionary communism') but increasingly also to refer to the beliefs of mainstream political parties ('the ideology of the Conservative Party', 'the ideology of the Republican Party'). These senses of ideology can fit into the above model if they are seen as descriptive of one consequence of the ideological process – beliefs which are held consciously and which are believed to have been arrived at rationally. Just as Freud believed that the conscious mind was the tip of the mental iceberg, with the much larger part remaining hidden in the unconscious, so consciously held political beliefs are the tip of the unconscious ideological structures which operate within us. The broader sense of ideology thus puts these beliefs in a larger context and undermines their claim to conscious rationality.

The functions of ideology

So far we have given only an outline of the nature of ideology. To arrive at a more detailed picture, we can ask what are the causes and functions of ideology. In the traditional Marxist account, ideology has a purely economic cause. A specific economic structure (for example, capitalism) gives rise to a specific social structure (for example, a class system) and this social structure gives rise to particular ways of thinking. Thus the economic base is the cause of the ideological superstructure. A particular ideology is caused by a particular socio-economic system. The function of ideology is the perpetuation of this system. This is performed most effectively by making the system seem natural, god-given, or ideal, so that the

subordinate classes accept it without question. Althusser expresses
this in the following way.

> The reproduction of labour power requires not only a reproduction of
> its skills, but also, at the same time, a reproduction of its submission
> to the rules of the established order, i.e. a reproduction of submission
> to the ruling ideology for the workers, and a reproduction of the
> ability to manipulate the ruling ideology correctly for the agents of
> exploitation and repression.[14]

There are several problems with this account. It seems to indicate: 1.
that ideology is totally determined by the economic structure, 2. that
the possibility of ideological change is limited to the occurrence of
economic change, and 3. that members of subordinate classes must
totally accept (that is, believe) the ideology of the dominant class.
We will deal with each of these points in turn.

That ideology is totally determined by the economic system seems
to be implied by the base/superstructure model with its insistence
that everything depends on the base, as a house depends on its
foundations. However, this model has been seen as too simplistic,[15]
not least by Althusser himself who suggested that the superstructure
has a 'relative autonomy'. In other words, ideology is not simply a
distorted reflection of the economic structure but has a certain
amount of independence, allowing the possibilities of ideology being
changed by other elements in the superstructure, and of ideology
itself being a cause of economic change. Rather than a superstructure resting on a base, economic structures and ideological
structures should be seen as intertwined frameworks of social
action. Changes in one result in changes in the other. Economic
change results in ideological change, but this latter change can itself
lead to further economic change. The economy and ideology should
not be seen as discrete entities, but rather as theoretical abstractions
from a complex social totality.

Although this deals with the first two points mentioned earlier, we
are still left with the third, the subordinate class's acceptance of the
dominant ideology. Members of a subordinate class will find themselves in a potentially contradictory situation. On the one hand, they
live in a society structured by a dominant ideology. On the other
hand, their own particular economic situation will give rise to a
particular set of concerns which may differ radically from that of
the dominant class. One of the features of class difference is that
different social classes may have different ways of understanding the
world, that is, different ideologies. Rather than subordinate classes
having to accept totally the dominant ideology (which would put
severe pressures on that ideology), they only need to accept part of

it, in particular that part which legitimizes the socio-economic structure.

Gramsci and hegemony

The Italian Marxist Antonio Gramsci (1891–1937) is a useful writer to refer to at this point in the discussion. He suggested that in order to retain its hegemony (that is, its moral and political claims to leadership) the dominant class will articulate (that is, join on to its own concerns) some of the aspirations of the subordinate classes, thus incorporating elements from the subordinate ideologies into the dominant ideology.[16] The dominant class gives a little, in order to retain a lot. The extension of the right to vote in Britain during the nineteenth and twentieth centuries is an example. Desire for political change is defused by the dominant class gradually giving up its monopoly of electoral power, while at the same time retaining its central role in society (and, incidentally, expanding its own membership). Another example is the gradual widening of the range of broadcast material on British radio, from the BBC's origin in the 1920s, through the popular wartime services for the armed forces, and on to the creation of Radio One as a popular music channel in 1967. The expansion of content, moving away from the BBC's elitist and patrician origins towards a more demotic form of broadcasting (while retaining a minority 'high' culture channel on Radio Three) can be seen as a Gramscian process of articulation. The BBC's position of cultural dominance is preserved, while the programming is opened up to satisfy some of the desires of the population at large.

This model of hegemony and articulation suggests that ideological struggle is a continuing feature of any society in which one social group has dominance over another. Class differences in themselves produce ideological forces of change, exerting pressures across the superstructure. In addition to this it is important to retain a sense of the real differences between people, even those brought up in the same social context. Freud's model of psychic development, seeing individuals as involved in unique, if similar, dramas of maturation, is useful here. Each person has to negotiate his or her own route through the processes of sexual desire and sexual differentiation. Freud termed the most important phase of these processes as the Oedipus Complex, the phase in which sexual identity is confirmed by a dialectical relationship with the parents. Each person's journey from birth (and dependence on the mother) to adult independence of both parents is unique, occurring in a unique situation. For example, the Oedipal drama may determine one person to accept uncritically the authority of the dominant ideology, but may determine another to rebel against it. Add to this regional variations (to be born into the middle class in a large city may produce a different relationship to the dominant ideology from being born into the middle class in a remote rural community) and we get a sense of the ideological complexities found in even a small industrial nation. All that is needed for the dominant ideology to function is for there to be sufficient ideological overlap within the dominant class and sufficient hegemony over the other classes. Thus the total structure of the dominant ideology is likely to be contradictory and fragmentary, rather than coherent and unified.

Conclusion

Ideology, then, can be seen as a complex process by which our experience of the world is structured. Its source lies in our own socio-economic origins. It functions to reproduce that originating condition. The patterns of power in society are repeated in ideology, with the ideology of the powerful being the dominating form of understanding in any society. An ideology is not, however, a simple, undifferentiated structure, but a complex of overlapping and sometimes contradictory elements articulated together. Rather than being inherently powerful and difficult to avoid, it is, on the contrary, a structure of variable strength which, when interacting with individuals, can result in a variety of positions.

It might be thought that the view of ideology suggested here is too broad. As a general rule, the wider the application of a concept, the less analytically useful it becomes (definitions of 'culture' run the same risk). Its analytical force, however, can be preserved by emphasizing ideology's role as an unconscious stabilizer and justifier of the status quo. It can be used to make clear the distinction between 'natural', 'commonsense' and 'obvious' views and the class-weighted, socially produced beliefs and practices which we all, to some extent, have and need.

Our next step will be to look a bit more closely at ideological processes and their effects

2 Processes and effects

In order to broaden the detail of the description given in chapter 1, it will be useful to consider in more depth the processes involved in ideology. Some writers have put the whole emphasis on this aspect. Thus Sylvia Harvey writes of 'the great disadvantage of presenting ideology as an entity, a quantity, a thing, rather than as a process, an operation, a kind of work'.[1] Such an approach has the advantage of not only emphasizing the processes involved in, for example, cultural products themselves, but also the processes involved in the way the audience experiences such products.

It was noted earlier how the process of ideology involves the production of meaning and of subjectivity. John Fiske was quoted at the beginning of the previous chapter, describing ideology as 'the social production of meaning'. Elsewhere he has defined it as 'the social relations of signification (knowledge and consciousness) in class societies'[2] and more specifically as 'the production and distribution of ideas in the interests of the ruling classes'.[3] The emphasis on meaning and signification is useful, despite this definition's too narrow limitation to 'the ruling classes'. Such an emphasis draws attention to two aspects of the ideological process – the creation and the interpretation of signs. By 'signs' is meant everything which stands for something else in a social situation, including words (spoken or written), symbols, images, gestures and sounds. Such signs become meaningful by being used according to specific codes and conventions. These codes and conventions are the rules by which we are able to generate meaning. If meaning is essentially social (which it must be if we are able to communicate with other people) then ideology – as the structure of the social – must be involved. But the moment of 'decoding' (when the individual interprets the signs) is also ideologically important, being the moment at which the individual brings his or her own ideological formation into play. Thus every stage of the passage from cultural producer through mediated text to audience member is heavily implicated in any comprehensive theory of ideology.

Subjectivity

The concept of decoding suggests that the ideological product is affected by the consumer, but the idea of subjectivity suggests another process – the cultural product as addressing, and in some sense creating, a specific audience. In order to understand a cultural text or event, the consumer puts her or himself in the position to which the text or event is addressed. 'Text' is here being used in a very broad sense as any non-transitory or semi-permanent cultural product which offers itself to an audience of consumers – it includes written texts, audio-visual texts such as films and television programmes, embodied texts such as buildings, and even such structured cultural products as hairstyles and clothing. 'Event' covers any transitory or non-permanent performance in time and includes sporting, theatrical and religious events, among others.

Althusser used the term 'interpellation' to describe the way in which ideology 'calls out' to individuals. The text, then, is a structured product which calls out to an audience, attempting to elicit a specific reaction. This is most clearly demonstrated in the system of point-of-view in visual texts (the camera places us in a particular relationship with what appears on the screen, and frequently invites us to identify with fictional characters). It also works in many other ways. Religious rituals put us in particular relationships with divinities; presenters and commentators talk directly to us; sporting events are often constructed for a large audience which is assumed to have specific interests; and many buildings are designed to have a certain effect on people as they walk in and around them. For Althusser, every time we 'accept' the interpellated 'call' of an ideological product (that is, every time we position ourselves as the text asks), we thereby confirm our own ideological situation.

Some further examples should help to make this notion of subjectivity and ideological address clearer. At a straightforward level, any use of written or spoken language will imply both a source and an audience. We, as members of the audience, may not know the source, or may make mistaken assumptions about it, but if language is being used, then it is being used *by* someone, and that person has some intention in using it. A simple example is a road sign, saying, for example, 'Danger'. The precise authorship of this sign is irrelevant. The message is very conventional. The important source, as far as road users are concerned, is the group of people with knowledge of the situation and authority to do something about it. The road sign, then, is addressed by someone. But it is also addressed *to* someone – in this case, a fairly large and mixed group consisting of all users of that specific stretch of road. Where, then, do ideology and subjectivity enter into the situation? The sign makes a number of assumptions about its readers. It assumes that they know enough about roads to understand the kind of danger being signalled. It also assumes that they are in a position to do something about it, and that they would want to do something about it. These may seem obvious enough conditions but it is not difficult to imagine a society in which they do not hold. Thus values and judgments are entering into the functioning of even this very simple communication. A particular type of human being is assumed, and as we react to the sign, slowing down our car speed, we are, in effect, accepting the assumptions as valid. We are confirming the account of human subjectivity which is implied by the road sign. This is a very simple example, and one which could fit into many ideological systems, but when we move to more complex texts and more complex modes of address, then the subjectivity becomes more focused, and the ideological implications become more specific.

This notion of being subject to ideological address and, through our response to it, continually confirming and maintaining our ideological status, has aroused a good deal of debate. Some writers (such as Paul Hirst) have argued that our subjectivity cannot be constituted by ideology since, logically, it must predate any specific instance of ideological address – we must be able to recognize ourselves as identifiable human subjects before being able to respond to any particular ideological text.[4] This argument depends on subjectivity being *only* an ideological effect. If, on the other hand, we see ideological subjectivity as simply one *form* of subjectivity, that is, just one way in which human subjectivity is reproduced, then pre-ideological subjectivity is possible. We can see subjectivity as a psychic formation originating in the earliest years of life. Freud's notion of the Oedipus Complex as the process by which we become socialized (that is, become ideological subjects) is useful here (as noted in the previous chapter). Ideological subjectivity then becomes part of a continual process of subject formation. This can be put another way by noting the distinction between a non-self-conscious subjectivity (the self as a centre of action) and a self-conscious subjectivity (the self as the answerer of ideological interpellations). We grow from the former to the latter as we mature into socialized adults.

Another criticism has been that this concept of subjectivity does not seem to allow for any change or conflict. Stuart Hall makes this argument as follows.

> It is . . . conceptually impossible to construct, from this position, an adequate concept of 'struggle' in ideology, since (for example) struggle against patriarchal ideology would be a struggle against the very repressive conditions in which language as such is itself constituted.[5]

That is, if we are interpellated as subjects, and this subjectivity has a deep psychic level of formation, implicit in our roles as language users, it becomes difficult to see how we can escape this ideological structuring. The answer to this is to note how fragile subjectivity can be. We must always be ideological subjects if we are to be recognizably human and participate in social discourse, but the various discourses and processes which construct subjectivity can produce contradictory subject positions and we can, of course, answer the interpellation in different ways, even to the extent of outright rejection (which may happen if we recognize the subjectivity on offer as conflicting with our own self-image, like an atheist in a church congregation). Subjectivity is never a completed process (after all, we are continually growing, experiencing and trying to make sense of life). It is always needing to be constructed anew. Having said that, it must be noted that most interpellation will, to some extent at least, overlap so that major ideological changes are not likely, even though they are possible.

Ideological effects

Discussion of subjectivity leads us on to the more general question concerning the effects of ideology. After all, the justification for studying ideology is that it is important in our lives, that is, that it has important effects. To begin with, it is worth emphasizing that the maintenance of ideology is a long-term process. Although it is most convenient to study its workings in very specific contexts – a particular event, product, or practice – we can deduce very little about general effects from such isolated and specific analyses. More important are the long-term effects – not just how one television programme affects its audience, not even how television in general works, but rather how the whole cultural complex affects us. When this is added to the audience's decoding activity, then it becomes clear that the strongest effect is likely to be that of reinforcement, rather than conversion. This is a fairly obvious point to make but is a necessary one because of the tendency of some writers to make general deductions from very limited examples. Only if it is assumed that all ideology is the same can such deductions carry weight, but this has already been shown to be an unwarranted assumption.

Looking at effects generally, we can follow Kenneth Thompson and suggest two major ways in which ideology can work – as social cement and as social control.[6] To see ideology as social cement is to see it as the force which binds society, providing the framework in which social action can take place. To see ideology in terms of social control, on the other hand, is to see it as having a more direct and coercive effect on social actors, thus emphasizing its function of policing the class formations of the social structure. Rather than seeing these as alternatives, we should see them as two aspects of ideological effect, whose relative importance will vary with changing circumstances. However, it is worth adding that the very real ideological conflict which frequently occurs in democratic capitalist societies suggests that the social control aspect is at best only partially successful. States dominated by religion, such as Iran, are perhaps the clearest examples of the the social control effect. This leaves the emphasis, in democratic societies, on social cement. Subjectivity fits into this as the process by which social positions are created and maintained, a crucial element in the process of ideological 'cementing.'

It is, however, important to avoid simplifying and overestimating the power of ideology. There must be room for different reactions to the same ideological statement, whether it is explicitly political or woven into the fabric of some cultural practice, and in this context it is useful to consider Frank Parkin's account of the three ways in which individuals can react to a dominant ideology.[7] The first is simply to accept the dominant account. Parkin argues that this leads to a deferential or aspirational attitude – we *defer* to the dominant understanding, and *aspire* to succeed within those terms. The second reaction is to accept a subordinate ideology (for Parkin, the typical example is that of a working-class community) seen by those within it as different from but inferior to the dominant ideology. This leads to an accommodative attitude – we *accommodate* such unpalatable situations as unemployment and inferior status. Parkin's third reaction is to accept a radical ideology, rejecting the dominant ideology and promoting an alternative. This leads to an oppositional attitude.

David Morley has used this approach in studying the television audience. He adapted Parkin's terminology to develop the notion of dominant, negotiated and oppositional ideological positions (which result in dominant, negotiated and oppositional readings of television programmes). The change from 'subordinate' to 'negotiated' is useful in that it moves the concept away from Parkin's strict class basis. For Morley, negotiation (and opposition) may come from a variety of sources apart from class, such as gender, occupation, age, and ethnic origin. This leads him to note 'the multiplicity of ideologies produced by the range of political parties and organisations within civil society.'[8] Such an approach can be a useful reminder of the potential variety of ideological response in any complex society.

A more comprehensive study based on similar premises is found in the work of John Fiske. In *Understanding Popular Culture* and *Reading the Popular*, he develops an audience-centred approach which emphasizes the ways in which ideology is resisted. He describes his work in the following terms.

Instead of concentrating on the omnipresent, insidious practices of the dominant ideology, it attempts to understand the everyday resistances and evasions that make that ideology work so hard and insistently to maintain itself and its values.[9]

Seeing ideology as a very imperfect tool for maintaining hegemony, he suggests that analysis should look at the ways in which texts can be used by people, rather than the opposite approach which looks at how people are used by texts.

The complementary focus is upon how people cope with the system, how they read its texts, how they make popular culture out of its resources. It requires us to analyze texts in order to expose their contradictions, their meanings that escape control, their producerly invitations; to ask what it is within them that has attracted popular approval.[10]

Fiske avoids going to the opposite extreme of seeing ideology as powerless, but emphasizes that ideological subjectivity can be refused or negotiated.

The people are not the helpless subjects of an irresistible ideological system, but neither are they free-willed, biologically determined individuals; they are a shifting set of social allegiances formed by social agents within a social terrain that is theirs only by virtue of their constant refusal to cede it to the imperialism of the powerful.[11]

It is important to note that Fiske is not arguing against theories of ideology or the usefulness of ideological analysis. Rather he is arguing that such theories and analyses are incomplete and need to be complemented by textual and audience studies which allow for a suitable variety of reaction. His discussions of, for example, video arcades, Madonna, and television news, form useful counterparts to the ideological analyses in our later chapters.[12]

Discursive ideologies and decentred subjects

At this point it is worth discussing a rather different approach to ideological subjectivity and effects. In *Uncommon Cultures*, Jim Collins outlines a theory of 'discursive ideologies'. This theory has been developed at greater length by Ernesto Laclau and Chantal Mouffe in *Hegemony and Socialist Strategy*[13] but Collins's more accessible version is useful here since he is specifically concerned with cultural study. He argues that the notion of a dominant ideology is now untenable since culture is clearly fragmented and we must instead consider ideology to be found in discourse, that is, in the many ways of speaking, understanding and acting which make up social life. Laclau and Mouffe describe a discourse as 'an articulatory practice which constitutes and organizes social relations.'[14] These discourses are self-legitimating and not tied down to social and economic factors. Collins expresses this in two statements.

> 1. No discourse may be considered innately superior in that it is more accurate, truthful, or scientific in its correlation with the world of objects;
> 2. Every discourse tries to deny this fact, and the assertion of its superiority is responsible for the creation of its own ideology.[15]

Thus the cause of ideology is discursive competition. Each discourse interpellates subjects but competing discourses will interpellate us in contradictory ways. In such a culture we become 'decentred' subjects without a unifying, coherent identity. Nevertheless, according to Collins, we are still able to exercise choice between these various discourses.

There are various problems with this. It becomes difficult to justify retention of the word 'ideology' when the break with socio-economic context is so complete – here there is not even Althusser's insistence on determination 'in the last instance'. There is no account of how subjects are formed able to choose between discourses. If we really are fragmented, decentred ideological subjects then such ability to choose seems unlikely, since the concept of personal identity loses much of its meaning. It will also be clear that Collins's rejection of the dominant ideology is based on a very simplistic, monolithic account. Rather than trying to refine that account, he goes to the opposite extreme, throwing out the baby with the bathwater. Finally, it is not clear on this account that ideology serves any purpose, since subjects can choose and reject interpellation so easily. In effect Collins moves completely away from the concept of ideology, but can only do this by basing his argument on a caricatured version of the opposing argument and on a highly selective and contentious description of contemporary culture. The most useful aspect of his account is the emphasis he puts on the variety of ideological address with which we are confronted. This clearly has important consequences but there is no reason to extend these to the complete abandonment of any non-discursive ideological formations (although for Laclau and Mouffe *everything* is constituted by discourse and the non-discursive is an empty concept).[16] Rather it should be seen as allowing greater ideological negotiation, but this negotiation implies a centred subjectivity, rather than a fragmentary one. We may adopt multiple subject positions without thereby losing a centred identity.

The epistemological status of ideology

Finally, we will consider the epistemological status of ideology, that is, the question of what kind of knowledge is ideological knowledge. Some kinds of knowledge claim to be based on experience (empirical knowledge). Some claim to be based on logical definitions (mathematics would be an example). Others claim to be based on authority (such as religious authority guaranteeing the status of scriptural texts), or on some kind of intuition (moral and aesthetic statements are sometimes given this foundation). In our society, scientific knowledge is still routinely thought to be the most respectable form of knowledge, based as it is on a combination of experience and a particular method (the experimental method, which is based not on whether statements can be proved to be true, but on whether they can be proved to be false). The classic Marxist position is that ideology is a distorted (not simply false) view of reality, and is contrasted with objective, scientific knowledge. A strong statement of this view is presented in Terry Lovell's *Pictures of Reality*. As noted in the previous chapter, she defines ideology as 'erroneous beliefs whose inadequacies are socially motivated'.[17] The problem with this is that it makes it impossible to formulate adequate criteria for the identification of non-ideological knowledge. If one of the hallmarks of ideology is its seeming obviousness, then simple claims to scientific objectivity stand in need of further justification. The logical problem is that we need to know what non-ideological knowledge is before we can establish criteria for it, but without the criteria such knowledge is unjustifiable. Appeals to scientific method are unavailing. Paul Feyerabend has suggested that scientific method itself is heavily implicated by ideology, favouring certain types of knowledge over others.[18] We are left with the problem which David McLellan describes.

> For the simple thought that all views are ideological encounters two difficulties: first, that it borders on the vacuous, since it is so all-embracing as to be almost meaningless; secondly, and more damagingly, it contains the same logical absurdity as the declaration of Epimenides the Cretan who declared that all Cretans were liars.[19]

Despite McLellan's use of the vague term 'views', this argument covers both beliefs and claims about the status of knowledge. The first point he makes has already been answered in the previous chapter when it was noted that, even if all views are ideological, it can still be analytically useful to show how such views are related to their causes, and also the degree to which they are determined by those causes. Not all views may be ideological in the same way and to the same extent.

The second point can be dealt with by noting that the logical absurdity of the Cretan liar paradox is *not* in fact the same as the logic of the statement about ideology. The paradox of the liar is created by the fact that the statement 'all Cretans are liars', when said by a Cretan, is false if it is true, and true if it is false. It is a straightforward example of a logical contradiction. The statement 'all views are ideological' only has the same logic if it is based on a view of ideology which sees all ideology as totally false, not merely distorted, and which does not allow for any degrees of variation in ideological determination. If 'all views are ideological' is taken to mean 'all views are false' then it *is* like the liar paradox. But we have already rejected such a narrow account.

Conclusion

In this introductory survey of theories of ideology, we have seen how the creation and maintenance of subjectivity is an important concern of ideology, and how varied are the effects of ideology. It will be clear from this that the task of identifying ideological effects is an immensely difficult one. More useful is the task of studying cultural products in order to trace their ideological determinations. This will at least give us a view of the main possibilities of ideological reaction which they (and, beyond the individual texts and events, the culture at large) present. The next problem is therefore to make the link between these fairly abstract theoretical concerns and the concrete phenomena of cultural production. That will be done in chapter 3 by looking at methods of ideological analysis.

3 Methods of analysis

When approaching the topic of ideological analysis it is useful to concentrate on cultural products. These products – in the form of both texts and events, as defined in the previous chapter – are clearly identifiable and are thus more amenable to analysis than social institutions such as the family or the educational system. To clarify what is meant by *cultural product*, however, it is necessary first to define *culture*. This is as complex to define as ideology, but a useful guide to its various definitions can be found in Raymond Williams's *Keywords*.[1] As he notes, in origin it refers to something which is grown (as in agriculture, or horticulture) and this sense of an outgrowth of society is a useful one to hold on to. Williams notes that in historical and cultural studies it is used to refer to 'signifying or symbolic systems'.[2] It would include all those artefacts and codes (for example, of dress, design, speech, or behaviour) which communicate meaning to us in some way, even if not consciously. Fiske suggests that

> Culture consists of the meanings that we make of social experience and of social relations, and the pleasures, or unpleasures, we find in them.[3]

Rather than referring to all aspects of a society, then, we can limit culture to those aspects which have a place in any system of symbolic meaning. *Culture* refers to the sum total of such elements in a society. *Cultural products* refers to specific, identifiable objects and events in which the culture is made manifest. This should clarify the relationship between culture and ideology. The culture of a society is a material manifestation of ideology. In this sense, culture can be seen as ideology in action – ideology given a specific expression. The analysis of cultural products then becomes a convenient way in which to study ideology. Our aim in this chapter is therefore to suggest methods for studying how ideology works in such texts and events.

Despite having been on the critical agenda for at least the last twenty years, there are remarkably few general guides to the ideological analysis of culture. The first, and still the most stimulating, work of this kind is Roland Barthes's *Mythologies*, first published in 1957 (although only reaching an English translation in 1972). Analysing a very wide range of materials (cookery, car design, striptease, wrestling) Barthes shows how they manifest *myth*, which he defines as a system of communication which makes the artificial seem natural.[4] It is thus one aspect of ideology. Typically some creation of human society is transformed into the semblance of absolute, non-human nature, and thus is removed from the realm of argument. A wrestling match is transformed into an elemental, natural conflict. A new car becomes a sign of transcendent spirituality. The problem with Barthes's technique is that it is essentially intuitive and dependent on the perspicacity of the analyst. Despite his use of the seemingly scientific terminology of semiotics, he does not display a method which can be followed easily.

Another approach is that of Fredric Jameson who sees the ideological analysis of cultural texts as being the identification of single beliefs and values, or (the more likely alternative in many cultural products) *protonarratives*, that is, the minimal dramatic elements which form the foundations of any narrated fiction.[5] These beliefs, values and protonarratives he calls *ideologemes*, defined as 'the smallest intelligible unit of the essentially antagonistic collective discourses of social classes'.[6] When the text is seen as a symbolic act it can be interpreted as the site of conflicting discourses in which ideologemes can be traced. Jameson then goes on to describe the primary task of ideological analysis.

> The analyst's work is thus first that of the identification of the ideologeme, and, in many cases, of its initial naming in instances where for whatever reason it had not yet been registered as such.[7]

This notion of the minimal meaningful unit of ideology is an attractive one, although when actually put to the test it can be as difficult and controversial to isolate as Barthes's myths. The concept of the protonarrative, however, will be worth remembering when we come to analyse narrative texts. It indicates the importance of avoiding limiting our analysis to the more obvious aspects of content, such as beliefs and value judgments. Also useful, even if only as a reminder, is Jameson's motto – 'always historicize!' – which he describes as 'the one absolute and we may even say "transhistorical" imperative of all dialectical thought'.[8] It is clearly derived from Barthes's notion of ideology as that which tries to naturalize the historical. The process of analysis, then, will in part retrace this process and attempt to historicize the seemingly natural and to show its artificiality.

Such a broad imperative does not, however, take us very far when we want to analyse a particular cultural product. For this a more detailed approach is required. In order to attempt this, five categories of analysis will be described. This is not to lay down some fundamental method which must always be followed, but rather to indicate areas of importance which should repay attention. As will be clear in the analyses later in this book, the relative importance of these categories will vary in different cultural phenomena. The five categories are content, structure, absence, style, and mode of address.

Content

Content is an extremely broad and general category covering all the more obvious aspects of cultural products. Four elements in particular can be noted: judgments, vocabulary, characters and actions. The first consists of the explicit statements made in the course of the text or event. We are here talking about assertions, opinions, denials, etc., rather than the descriptive language used. Beliefs and values are likely to be a fairly obvious and, indeed, self-conscious part of this sub-category. Of all aspects of cultural texts, this is, by its very nature, the most readily appreciated. When audiences are asked about the ideological content of cultural texts, this is the category to which they are most likely to refer.

The second element of content, and one which is very closely related to the first, is the vocabulary used. By this is meant principally the choice of descriptive language. The ideological implications of this will be most obvious in arguments such as whether particular groups should be referred to as 'freedom fighters' or as 'terrorists'. However, the question is much broader than this example might indicate. The choice of adjective in any description carries value judgments with it. This is not limited simply to linguistic aspects of the cultural text itself. It can be expanded to include what are called *secondary texts*. If the cultural phenomena themselves can be regarded as primary texts, then discussions of them (criticism, commentary, description) can be seen as secondary texts. Thus even non-linguistic cultural phenomena may have secondary texts attached to them (such as newspaper and magazine articles) in which they are described in linguistic terms. Such secondary texts may come to play a crucial role in circulating definitions and evaluations of cultural products. An obvious example of this is broadcast and print commentary on sporting events. This should alert us to the need to analyse cultural products in their setting (which includes the secondary texts) rather than in isolation. It also, incidentally, points out the predominant role of the mass media in cultural matters.

The third aspect of content consists of the characters which may be represented in the cultural product, including stereotyped characters. The kind of person who appears in fiction and how that person is portrayed are the most obvious examples, but this sub-category extends far beyond fiction. Sporting commentaries are frequently organized around stereotypes (the young and innocent player, the dirty player, the player past his or her prime, etc.) and famous characters will often take on heroic or villainous functions. Similarly news reports frequently feature stereotyped heroes and villains. Real people are made to fit character roles in order to protect ideological homogeneity. Reality becomes an illustration of ideology.

The final element of content consists of actions. A dominating category in sport, this will clearly have a very close link to characters, and just as characters are frequently stereotyped, so are actions. Think of the typical actions in a Western film, or the typical gestures in a football match (such as those of celebration, despair, or disbelief). Actions express and resolve the conflicts of the text or event. They become the high points, the points of greatest involvement and pleasure for the audience.

The ideological importance of these four sub-categories of content is that they are used to express a view of reality – a view which the audience is asked to share. We, as readers/viewers/listeners (even participants), are not forced to share this view but, if we want to get the pleasure and sense of shared identity which cultural products promise, then we must, at least for a short time, accept their perspective on the world.

Structure

Content does not stand alone and part of the meaning of any element of a cultural product derives from its position within the whole artefact. This should be obvious in the case of any work of fiction, but it is also true of any hierarchically arranged phenomenon. One example would be news reporting, in which order of delivery implies order of importance. Another example would be a competitive game, in which any incident (such as a score being made) gets its meaning from its relation to what has gone before (the score may be an equalizer, a winner or a consolation score for the loser). This can be termed *diachronic structure* – that is, a structure which is manifested in the temporal ordering of a phenomenon. A comes before B, which in turn comes before C. We, as audience, experience A first, followed by B, and ending with C.

Although any position within a structure carries meaning, particularly important are the opening and closing elements. The opening serves to declare the agenda, to set limits on the content. It sets the 'problem' which the text answers (which may be a very specific question in a narrative fiction, such as who was the murderer, or may be a question of who – or which side – is superior, as in sporting events, or may be a general question such as what important events have happened in the last twelve hours). The essential point of ideological interest is that the opening declares the purpose of the text or event. Similarly the closing of the text or event signifies the closing of the problem, the answering of the relevant questions. An open-ended structure (such as in some forms of fiction) will generally allow for a far greater freedom of interpretation and thus avoid *ideological closure*, in which the possibilities of meaning are restricted to a relatively narrow range. The opening and closing moments define a structure, giving a framework. Although a non-temporally ordered phenomenon, such as a photograph, cannot be said to have a beginning or an end, it does have a boundary, literally a frame, which gives it order and limits the scope of its structure. This makes very clear the importance of the everyday newspaper practice of cropping photographs, thus manipulating their meaning by altering their content and emphasis.

Television news gives a clear example of a non-fictional but highly structured form. Typically, it opens with the announcement of purpose ('Here is the news'), then defines its structure by giving the headlines, and after a carefully ordered progression of stories, often ends with a less 'serious' item and usually a summary rounding off, sometimes even closing by echoing the opening announcement ('That was the news'). This structuring gives an order to events which is independent of the specific items mentioned. It is a closed structure, adaptable to any happening in the world, able to incorporate it into its ordered version of reality. It imposes ideological clarity ('This is how things are') to an inherently unclear situation.

Another form of structure is that which is implied by the distinctions made or assumed by the text. Typically these will take the form of oppositions between two elements, such as good and bad, old and young, male and female, dark and light, capitalist and communist, powerful and weak, etc. These may form a deep level of structure, discovered by analysing the content of the text. Because of their form they are often referred to as *binary oppositions* and they give a structure which can be called *synchronic*. A synchronic structure is implied throughout the text rather than developing in a linear manner as in a diachronic structure. It is an opposition of terms, and thus of values, being the ground out of which meaning is generated. Ronald Reagan's famous reference to the Soviet Union as 'the Evil Empire' only becomes fully understandable as part of an implied opposition which contrasts the Soviet Union with the United States. The Evil Empire is contrasted with the Good Nation, the Defender of the Free World. Within such a scheme, Reagan's comment becomes not only unremarkable, but simply a statement of the obvious. Outwith such a scheme, however, it becomes simply abuse of a rival country. Examples of such oppositional categories can usually be found without too much difficulty in any news programme, as another level of structure alongside the diachronic.

Absence

By its very nature this is a difficult category to deal with since its scope is potentially infinite. It can be made more manageable by regarding the absences (the elements which are missing from the text) rather as *avoidances*, that is, elements which might have been expected to be in the text but which are missing from it. The obvious problem here is that an evaluative judgment (which is itself ideological) creeps into the argument. How do we agree on what has been avoided in a text? More than any other category this one must remain at the level of probability. That does not, however, render it unusable. Consider the following examples. A work of fiction which claims to represent everyday life has no important female characters. A news report which claims to give all the day's news of importance in fact only covers political, economic and sporting news, and deals with all of these in terms of famous personalities. Such examples (and no doubt the reader can multiply instances of them) show how this category can work. It depends partly on working out what the text is claiming (however implicitly) to represent.

The French writer Pierre Macherey developed the notion of a *structuring absence* to describe how elements which are avoided can have a major determining effect on a text.

> The speech of the book comes from a certain silence, a matter which it endows with form, a ground on which it traces a figure. Thus, the book is not self-sufficient; it is necessarily accompanied by a *certain absence*, without which it would not exist. A knowledge of the book must include a consideration of this absence.[9]

Thus the absence is crucial to the work's ideological structure. Macherey goes on to compare it to Freud's notion of the unconscious – an essential part of the mind but one which is by definition unknown to consciousness. By this account, a structuring absence will be a crucial element in any cultural product. It virtually becomes the *raison d'être* of the text, that which it is constructed to avoid (rather like a by-pass – a road built specifically to avoid a place but which only exists because of that place).

An influential film analysis which makes much use of this category is that of the 1939 Hollywood film *Young Mr Lincoln*, directed by John Ford.[10] Originally written in French by the editors of the film magazine *Cahiers du Cinéma* in 1969, it discusses the version of President Lincoln's early career which the film presents and notes how it avoids two crucial areas – sexuality (despite showing Lincoln's love for Ann Howard) and politics (despite being the biography of a politician). The importance of these absences is that by avoiding them the film can construct a mythic view of Lincoln as the superhuman unifier of the nation. This should make clear the ideological importance of absences. It is not simply a matter of avoiding some issues, but rather of enabling the ideological argument of the text to be worked out unproblematically.

Style

Style is a rather vague concept but it can be outlined as what remains after the more obvious aspects of content have been dealt with. 'More obvious' since style is, to a certain extent, an aspect of content. However, it can usefully be distinguished from content by regarding it as the ways in which the content is made to cohere, apart from the structural aspects already considered. It can include the use of colour in pictures, the use of the camera in films, decorative elements in theatre, styles of verbal language, architectural settings (for example for sporting events), and many other features. They are features which are not explicit in the manner of linguistic content, and which do not function as major structural elements. However, they may share functions with other categories. Style can be read as a statement, and can be used to give a subtle structuring effect. In some cases (such as clothing fashions) style and content overlap completely. In other cases (such as television news) style overlaps importantly with structure. It has most independence from other elements in what is usually known as 'high art.' (It could be used as one of several definitional qualities of such art).

Of all these categories, style may seem to be the least involved with questions of ideology, but three examples should dispel this misapprehension. The first is literary style. Ernest Hemingway's books are well known for their seemingly objective style. This gives a particular resonance to the stories which he tells. A style which seems only to describe factually is used to construct specific fictions with specific themes. A second example is that of film lighting. Some films (most famously the Holywood crime films of the middle and late forties, known as *film noir*) use only a little lighting, creating very dark, shadowy images. This can easily be used metaphorically as a representation of a dark, dangerous and decaying society, even if the specific story seems to contradict this. A third example, getting away from fiction, would be a football match. Part of the style is the colours worn by the rival teams. Another aspect is the general behaviour of the players. These become important parts of the spectacle of the occasion, helping to transform a routine sporting event into something which seems to transcend everyday life. The historical becomes the mythical, and the values which the game implies become naturalized.

Mode of address

This is not always a very obvious feature of texts, and even less so of events, but nevertheless it is a crucial element. It concerns the way in which the cultural product is aimed at us, the way in which it 'speaks' to us. As mentioned in chapter 2, this is bound up with the notion of interpellation, that is, the way in which ideology creates audience positions by 'calling out' to us. Interpellation, and thus mode of address, attempts to confirm us as subjects situated within ideological structures. At its most obvious, it can be seen in the technique of *direct address*, for example in television programmes which speak to the audience in their homes. The presenter looks at the camera and addresses us directly. Advertisements of all kinds (audio-visual and print) are often clear examples of such direct address.[11] Many cultural products, however, use *indirect address*. An example is the way in which traditionally constructed fiction (whether filmed, televized, acted or written) ignores the presence of an audience (whether in a theatre, in the home, or in the form of the single reader) but yet, at the same time, is addressed precisely to such an audience. In direct address the ideological positioning is usually more obvious (and for that reason is typically used when the audience and the cultural producers are assumed broadly to be sharing an ideological position, with the most obvious example being televison news). Indirect address works to conceal the positioning of the audience and thus to situate viewers/readers/listeners within an ideology but without their explicit consent. It is therefore particularly suitable, in ideological terms, for working out a specific problem by giving it a fictional solution which the audience accepts, at least for the duration of the text's reading, in order to get the pleasure which the text offers. Popular films and television drama usually work in this way.

The contrast between direct and indirect is not the only distinction to be made when analysing mode of address. Another one is the distinction between *specific* and *general* address. By specific address is meant address to a very closely identified and limited audience. A specialist radio programme or magazine would be common examples. The presenter of a radio programme devoted to a particular kind of minority interest music may address his or her audience by making a lot of assumptions about their interests, assumptions which the casual listener may well not share. By general address is meant the attempt to address the totality of a nation, covering all ages, occupations, regions, genders, etc. The assumptions which such a mode of address must make are very different to those of the specialist programme.

A third distinction to be made is that between a *unified* mode of address and a *fragmented* one. This distinction will become clearer in the closing chapters of this book. At the moment it is enough to note that most cultural products will have a unified address, focused at one particular point (whether direct or indirect, specific or general) and those which do not will create differing, and possibly contradictory, positions for their audience. This fragmented address will tend to undermine any ideological certainties and thus will usually be a subversive technique within any cultural product. The best-known examples are probably the more experimental music videos in which images are mixed in a seemingly haphazard manner. (The notion of decentred subjectivity, discussed in the previous chapter, is sometimes used to describe the effect of such fragmented address – the images do not address a single, coherent subject position for the duration of the video.) However, the essentially commercial nature of music videos (being basically advertisements for a record) and the unifying function of the music tend to undermine any ideological subversiveness which is present in the imagery, as does the usual context of the viewing of these items – popular televison.[12]

That these distinctions are applicable to more than just the mass media can be seen by considering a football match. Here the address is usually indirect but occasionally direct (the audience is usually ignored but at moments of crisis or triumph participants may appeal to it). The address is also general, catering for anyone who cares to attend, and unified, since it does not create multiple viewing positions (it is assumed that all spectators are there for the same reason). If the game is televised, there will be an added commentary which will be a form of direct aural address, but the general and unified aspects will be retained (indeed they will probably both be strengthened).

Conclusion

To round off this discussion of methods of analysis, two points need to be stressed. The first is that the precise balance of these five elements will vary greatly among different kinds of cultural product. Some products may not involve some of these categories at all, or at least not to any significant extent. Also, to note these categories is only the beginning of analysis. The ways in which they work in any particular text or event still have to be determined by studying the cultural product itself. The intention here is simply to give a check-list of items worth considering.

The second point to be stressed is that we have been concerned here with only one limited aspect of the ideological process – namely, the construction of the text or event itself. To develop an analysis as convincingly as possible it must be linked, on the one hand, to the cultural position of the makers of the text, in order to demonstrate why such ideological forces may be at work; and on the other, to the intended audience. Texts do not force audiences into submission. As noted in the previous chapter when discussing the work of Frank Parkin, David Morley and John Fiske, audiences can read texts in many ways, including those which the producers may well regard as aberrant. To demonstrate the ideological forces at work in a cultural product is to do only that – demonstration of the audience's reaction must be made separately and cannot be assumed. This point will have particular importance in any society which is undergoing change and in which there is ideological con-flict. And as the events in Eastern Europe in 1989 have shown, even when a culture is dominated by a strong, seemingly unified ideology which has absolute power over the means of communication and cultural production, the audience may still be able to reject it.

We can now start the process of looking at how the ideological analysis of cultural products can be carried out in specific cases. Our selection will be made to demonstrate different methods and differ-ent problems of analysis, starting with a fairly straightforward example.

4 Advertising America

A suitable place to begin the ideological analysis of cultural products is the tourist industry, in particular the texts produced by it. These texts – typically in the form of holiday brochures – are designed to appeal directly to particular cultures. However, not every culture is involved in this industry. Tourism is, by and large, a feature of developed countries. A population needs to have reached a certain level of economic well-being before it can indulge in any kind of tourism. In many countries the notion of taking a holiday from work for a couple of weeks is completely foreign – all the more so the idea of using this time to travel to another country. Tourism, then, is not an innocent pastime. It signifies particular economic and social values. It is also a commercial endeavour. Tourist brochures are advertisements and, like all advertising, need to have an immediate impact. They are quite openly trying to sell something. In one sense, what they are selling is a country – or, at least, a particular view of particular parts of a country.

The specific example at which we will look is how the United States is described in some British holiday brochures. Examples will be taken from a representative, although certainly not complete, range of brochures, produced by British holiday companies for British tourists.[1] It is worth noting at the start that the cost of travelling across the Atlantic Ocean puts the United States in the upper range of holiday destinations for Britons. At the time of writing (Spring 1990) the cost of a fourteen-day self-catering holiday in Florida at the height of the tourist season was in the range of £550–£650, with destinations further west being proportionately more expensive. By contrast, the same kind of holiday in popular Mediterranean resorts such as the Greek Islands was in the range of £250–£350. This financial fact has implications for the target readership of the American brochures. They are aimed at an audience with above average income and who might therefore be expected to be more strongly integrated into the dominant value system in Britain. The implication of this is that they are also likely to be well integrated into the nation's symbolic system, that is, the system of mythic representations of the country, its people, and its history (or, at least, its history as it is mythologized, with kings, queens, heroes and battles well to the fore).

It should be noted that our concern here is simply with the descriptions of the United States. We are not concerned with the descriptions of specific hotels and apartments, nor with the illustrative material (although both of these categories could well be made an object of study). Our concern is simply to study the linguistic content in order to see how ideological themes are encoded into these texts. This is, of course, a fairly limited approach and would be inadequate if the intention was a complete analysis of these brochures, or of how the United States is represented in Britain. The aim here is the more restricted one of simply introducing the process of ideological analysis.

The greatest natural wonders

To begin with a very obvious theme, we will consider how scenery is described.

> The West's great National Parks with their cavernous echoing canyons, thundering waterfalls, snow-capped mountains and magnificent rugged grandeur are among the greatest natural wonders of the world.[2]

This is a fairly typical description of the wilderness areas of the American West. We can note its use of hyperbole – that is, its claim to be the 'greatest' in the world. Here is another example, taken from a different company's brochure.

> Bathed in sunshine, encompassing mountains and deserts, bounded by the rolling Pacific and the craggy peaks of the Rocky Mountain range, the West Coast of North America is one of the most spectacularly beautiful areas of the whole world.[3]

This appeal to extremes works by an implied contrast. Unstated is the added comment 'by contrast with Britain'. We are being asked to come to America in order to see a more dramatic scenery, a more extreme form of landscape, and one which we cannot, by implication, see at home. And just as many advertisements function by claiming that the advertised product is unique, and therefore desirable, so these descriptions function by implying that the scenery of the American West is worth seeing *because* it is unique – on a completely different scale from that of Britain, and even of Europe in general. The idea of uniqueness is brought out in another brochure by uniting the contradictory ideas of nature and art.

> The Grand Canyon, the seventh natural wonder of the world, stands unchallenged as nature's most remarkable work of art.[4]

The defining characteristic of human art – its originality – is applied to the natural world in an attempt to indicate the quality of unique difference which this holiday destination possesses.

Just as many advertisements include the desired reaction ('You'll be happier with our product'), so these descriptions frequently spell out the appropriate response.

> Visit Yellowstone Park – America's first, biggest and best known park – and witness the 'Old Faithful Geyser' erupt every 65 minutes, as it has done for over 100 years; marvel at the chameleon rock formations of Zion National Park, which change colour throughout the days and seasons; be awe-struck by the majestic, 14 mile wide, mile deep Grand Canyon. This a holiday packed with unforgettable sights and lasting memories.[5]

Worked into such writing is the assumption that this is what we go on holiday to see – something foreign, something unforgettable, something excessive by the standards of the home country. We travel looking for difference. But difference implies some standard of normality against which it can be measured.

It is not just the West which gets such a treatment. Consider this invitation to visit Florida.

> 'ISLAND OF FLOWERS.' That is what Ponce de Leon called it in 1513 because he thought he had discovered a huge island! Of course we know that it's really a peninsula way down south of the US of A and we also know that this gorgeous SUNSHINE STATE is just about the finest Holiday Destination in the world. OK we admit there are some other wonderful destinations in the world – but have they got EVERYTHING that FLORIDA has got? Take a near perfect climate. Add cooling Trade Winds. Surround by warm tropical seas, fill it with crystal clear lakes, the wonders of nature and wild life and then add the ingenuity of man to create Cities, Towns and areas designed solely for the comfort of living and leisure.[6]

Particularly interesting here is the combination of natural marvels with 'the ingenuity of man'. The excess and perfection of the scenery is carried over into human achievements so that the towns and cities become wonders to be seen as much as the natural features. This combination of the natural and the fabricated is made even more explicit in another brochure.

> The white sand and swaying palms of the South East Florida Gold Coast stretch from the colourful art deco area of historic Miami Beach way up to Fort Lauderdale – the Venice of Florida. The Everglades wilderness and the quaint Florida Keys to the south provide a perfect contrast to the man-made marvels elsewhere in the Sunshine State.[7]

Also of interest here is the final appeal to comfortable living with its implication that all towns and cities in Florida are devoted to this – no mention is made of the social problems of, for example, Miami. The entire state is painted as a paradise of luxurious living.

The other area to get this treatment as a place of excess is Hawaii.

> There are one hundred and thirty-two magical islands making up Hawaii and stretching sixteen hundred glorious miles across the Pacific. Some of them are just tiny dots in the Ocean while others have become favourite spots for a perfect holiday. Endless sunshine is complimented [*sic*] by gentle breezes carrying with them the perfume of flowers – gardenia, anthurium, plumeria and orchids. Brilliantly coloured birds live in lush green forests and graceful palm trees line wonderful sandy beaches.[8]

Here the excessive perfection becomes more explicitly paradisiacal with the promise of 'magical islands'. This text does, of course, make a lot of assumptions about 'the perfect holiday', virtually telling us what such a holiday should be. There is no notion here of individual holidays for individual people, just a blanket assumption of what everybody likes. Such a consensus implies not just what people are typically like, but also what human nature is like. It is simply 'commonsense' (the classic ideological marker) that there is such a thing as the 'perfect holiday' with which we would all agree.

Myth and history

By now another feature of these texts should be clear – their appeal to fundamental myths. The myth of the Lost Paradise is deeply embedded in the European consciousness and has, of course, biblical connotations. When we add to this the Celtic myth of a Land of Youth (*Tir nan Og*) across the Western sea, and other legendary places of magic, beauty and excess, then the mythic quality of these descriptions begins to become apparent. Barthes's idea of myth as the historical made natural (as noted in chapter 3) is useful here. These holiday destinations are historical in the sense that they can only function as contrasts to other places – places which are as they are in the late twentieth century. By contrast with the crowded regions of Europe and their smaller scale, visiting these American areas can seem to be a return to nature. A specific historical need – the desire for a particular kind of holiday contrast – is converted into a 'natural' desire for an ideal and somehow more 'real', although also more 'magical', world.

Another important theme running through these brochures is that of history. Some places are selected as being worth visiting for their historical associations. This is particularly true of Washington.

> George Washington chose the site for his City. It arose out of the swamps of the Potomac river. Unfortunately the naughty old British burnt it down in 1812! The peace saw a new city arise from the ashes.[9]

As with most countries, the history which is commemorated usually concerns the founding of the nation. The USA was, of course, founded by war with Britain – a fact which still seems to cause the brochure writers some embarrassment! The other historical period dealing with the formation of the modern USA is that of the Civil War, and this also gets the tourist treatment (even though this may be a history which is largely unknown to many Britons).

> Cross the State of New York into Pennsylvania, named for the father of the famous 'Quaker' William Penn. Enter the famous city of Gettysburg, site of the decisive battle of the Civil War. View the Confederate and Union fighting grounds, impressive burial memorials and location of Abraham Lincoln's famous Gettysburg address.[10]

Sometimes, however, the appeal to history covers less dramatic features more concerned with famous people than with famous events.

> Witness New England's romance with the sea today as you travel north to Salem's witch country. Lunch in Gloucester, where the Fishermen's Statue stands guard over the setting for Kipling's Captains Courageous. Watch the lobstermen at work and stop for a visit to Kennebunkport (where US President George Bush summers), as you travel the rugged coastline of Maine to Portland.[11]

It is interesting to note that for a British audience the Salem witch trials are best known through Arthur Miller's play *The Crucible*, and *Captains Courageous*, as well as being a story by Rudyard Kipling, is also known as a classic Hollywood film of 1938. Thus it begins to appear that the history being referred to is not so much the history produced from archives and documents, far less the history of how people lived and thought, but rather history as it appears in culture, represented and mythologized (that is, mediated by ideology) in literature, film and television.

The other area which is advertised by history is the South, in particular New Orleans which, with its European connections, makes an interestingly varied appeal.

> Flamboyant and magical. New Orleans is a city unto itself. Its unique carnival of cultures, inspired over a period of 250 years, has created a uniqueness which is uncommon to the rest of the USA. The Mississippi, Jazz, Mardi Gras and magical names such as Bourbon Street, Jackson Square and Pirates Alley are all to be found in the beating heart that is New Orleans.
>
> There are still streetcars, one named 'Desire', which transverse the districts of New Orleans. The French Quarter still retains the charm and vivacity of a historical community caught between the 19th and 20th century. Overhanging galleries and balconies reflect an era

influenced greatly by the French. In contrast to the quaintness of the French quarter the Central Business District reveals the new America of Skyscrapers and progress, full of dynamic energy.[12]

This quotation is interesting as a virtual summing up of themes already mentioned. It includes the notion of a magical place, and of New Orleans as a unique city signified by its excessive cultural mix. It refers to history, and to literature (Tennessee Williams's play *A Streetcar Named Desire* – also well-known in a 1951 film version), as well as making an explicit contrast with Europe.

The most exciting cities in the world

The previous extract also introduces a new but important theme – the idea of the United States as lively, energetic and fun-filled. This emerges most clearly in writing about the cities, especially New York.

> New York is one of the most exciting cities in the world. A city that never sleeps, it is unique, cosmopolitan and pulsating with vitality both day and night. New York has everything in abundance – entertainment, sightseeing, shopping, sports, culture – whatever your budget and tastes, you will never be bored.[13]

The link with the excessive description of scenery should be clear – New York as the excessive city with 'everything in abundance'. Similarly, Los Angeles is promoted for its excitement.

> Los Angeles, 'City of the Angels', is an enormous vibrant metropolis made up of 97 different towns – you'll certainly run out of time before you run out of things to do here![14]

As with New York, there is no mention of the city's massive social and economic problems. These are simply ignored or, occasionally, seen as another sign of excess in these 'vibrant metropolises'. Publicity for Las Vegas goes beyond that of the other cities by managing to link the excitement of the city with the magnificence of the scenery.

> Here you'll find an incredible range of entertainment in addition to the huge 24 hour casinos that have made Vegas so famous – as well as a great base from which to explore some of the most incredible natural sights in the world.[15]

As with earlier themes, this one works by an implied contrast, linked with an assumed desire. These cities are more exciting and more fun than British cities and therefore we must want to go there. When we recognize this hidden assumption of desire, then the idea that an account of human nature is assumed by these texts becomes more credible. To assume that human beings want particular things implies that human nature is of a particular kind.

Structure, absence and address

Although we have been talking about content, it should be clear that we have also been considering structure – not a diachronic structure, but a synchronic structure of binary oppositions (as described in chapter 3). The holiday destinations are set up as a set of contrasts with the home country. A particular place is advertised for a particular quality. The implication is that we want to go there because that quality is not possessed by our home region. Thus, as mentioned at the beginning of the chapter, the descriptions of the USA imply a set of opposing descriptions of Britain. These are not simply negative oppositions, however. If the American West is described as more grand and more spectacular, then Britain is by implication less grand and less spectacular, that is, more domestic and on a more personal scale. If New York and Las Vegas are more exciting and more fun, then British cities are, by implication, safer and quieter. If America has its history of the Revolution and the Civil War, Britain has its much longer history of kings, queens and battles. The appeal to one side of the oppositions implies a firm base in the other side.

By this time the absences in these brochures will be fairly obvious. Problems do not appear. Even the Civil War is mentioned simply as the cause of a few battles, rather than being a series of events with specific political, social and economic causes and effects. History appears simply as a museum with colourful contents which we can wander past and then forget. Race does not appear at all. Cold war militarism appears only very obliquely in comments about, for example, space exploration. Even the places mentioned imply the absence of all the other possible locations in the USA. There is no mention here of Pittsburgh, Detroit or Jersey City. As in any country, tourist resorts do not give a typical view. The advertising does not give any indication of this selectivity, frequently using language which hints towards the opposite – that all places in America are grand, historic or exciting, and that the destinations described are typical of the country. This signifies the United States as the country which has everything on a greater scale. Such a meaning is easily displaced on to politics and works ultimately to protect the country's position as leader of the Western world – it is signified as the greatest of nations and so deserving of its political hegemony.

It is worth making a brief comment here about the mode of address of these brochures. Typically they use a very direct form, often consisting of imperatives, such as 'See this', 'Visit that', 'Stay here', 'Drive there'. This, of course, is not unusual for advertising. Sometimes we are addressed by having our desires described ('Didn't you always want to visit Hollywood?'), in some cases in a very revealing way (as when they entice us to areas where the very rich live by suggesting that we can be like them). This is a form of interpellation, and one which we answer whenever we pick up such a brochure. On the other hand, since the texts are so short, and since in reading them we all have our own desires which may not match with those suggested by the copywriters, the overall ideological effect is likely to be weak. They will be most effective as reinforcements of ideological structures already with us – and of course the brochures are designed precisely to link up with the ways of thinking of their targeted audience.

All this may seem very far from the questions of social control and cohesion raised in the earlier chapters and so it is important that the links are made clear, particularly since tourism, compared with many activities, seems so innocent, and is now a near-universal practice in Britain. To make this link we need to note the view of Britain and the typical Briton which is implied by the binary oppositions of these brochures, and how these are linked (along with the whole institution of tourism) with the maintenance of the status quo. Those views are essentially 'safe' views, that is, they are based on what are seen as unchanging values of nationality and individuality – precisely the values which underpin the status quo. Thus the appeal of the United States as a tourist destination, in these brochures at least, is ultimately based on an appeal to a very traditional view of Britain, heavily coded as homely, domestic, unchanging, safe and, most importantly, normal. And the implication carries over into a view of the Briton as one who values the excessive excitements of America precisely because he or she is firmly rooted in such a context, with the 'normal' desires of a very British 'human nature'.

Conclusion

This chapter has served as a fairly simple introduction to ideological analysis. We have been concerned only with verbal texts, and have analysed these mainly through their descriptive language and synchronic structures. Such a process clearly has its limitations. Even the simplest tourist brochure will have a diachronic structure, that is, it will have a beginning, a middle and an end, and can be analysed according to the way this structure informs the content. However, tourist brochures, like most magazines, are frequently read by dipping into different sections, rather than by starting at the beginning and reading through to the end. Thus a synchronic analysis is more appropriate. Having said that, this kind of analysis does have its drawbacks. Pointing out binary oppositions is all very well when both terms of the opposition can be identified in the text. However, when one term is implied rather than stated (such as the view of Britain implied by these brochures) then the argument is on weaker ground. A different analyst (working from a different ideological position) might extrapolate a rather different version of the second term of the opposition. It is also the case, however, that the ideological force of such synchronic structures is correspondingly weaker than those which are more clearly identifiable.

5 Opening the wall

Tourist brochures are a fairly simple form of text. A more complex form, and one which by its very nature deals in politically controversial topics, is the newspaper. In this chapter we will look at news coverage of an important event to see how ideological analysis can be brought to bear on it. Examples from two countries – the United Kingdom and the United States – will be used. Both countries can be seen as working within broadly similar ideologies of capitalist democracy, even if there are significant differences of emphasis.

The analysis of newspaper reporting has its own problems. A newspaper is not a single, unified structure, but rather a multiplicity of different voices. A typical newspaper will include items by many different reporters (some acknowledged, some not), and these will be rewritten and adapted by unnamed sub-editors who will be responsible for the overall style and design of the paper. Some items will come directly from international news agencies, such as Reuters and UPI. Within stories there may be a variety of quoted voices, some named, some official, some credited as experts, some merely as witnesses. Precisely because it is not the voice of a single person, a newspaper makes an interesting object of analysis. It must also be remembered that newspaper publishing in Britain and the USA is a commercial activity. Most newspapers contain a lot of entertainment material (feature stories, reviews, cartoons) as well as a high percentage of advertising. And of course the news itself becomes a commodity which is used to sell the paper, particularly at the more popular end of the market. All of these factors mean that major newspapers are likely to be tied in very closely to the economic, political and social structures of their country of origin but may also allow a wide variety of voices to be heard.

Although there have been several ideological studies of newspapers,[1] the most comprehensive way to analyse news output is, of course, by a long-range study, building results from the way a newspaper is put together over a period of at least several months. The classic example of this method was produced by the Glasgow University Media Group in 1975, although it was concerned with television news rather than newspapers.[2] Here, however, such a large-scale study is not possible. Instead we will look at the coverage of one event in different newspapers to see what ideological forces may be at work. As with the other studies in this book, the intention is simply to show some of the ways in which ideological analysis can be carried out, rather than to make any hard and fast conclusions about the cultures in which these products were created.

Various features of newspapers can be considered as part of an ideological analysis. The way language is used, the way stories are structured, the amount of space and prominence given to any item, the use of headlines and of photographs are all worth considering. In addition, the function of the *by-line*, that is the statement of authorship, can be revealing. Our examples are two British newspapers and two from the United States. All of them can be considered as part of the 'élite' or 'quality' press. This selection is not, of course, typical of the texts which confront the majority of newspaper readers, but it does allow us to look at the more considered (and arguably more influential) press coverage, rather than the popular and sensational side. It will not allow us to make generalizations about news coverage (or even about the newspapers involved – for that we would need to look at many more editions) but it will allow us to see something of the ideological issues involved as we examine the rhetoric, vocabulary and design of these influential mediators.

The four newspapers are *The Times* and *The Independent*, both published in London, *The New York Times*, and *The Washington Post*. *The Times* has been long established as one of the leading media voices in Britain, often interpreted as the expression of the established power interests. During the 1980s it had been a consistent supporter of the Conservative government of Mrs Thatcher. *The Independent* is much younger, started in 1987 and established as the newspaper of the serious young professional, with a commitment to good design and a centrist political position which is not aligned with any particular party. *The New York Times*, with the largest editorial staff of any American paper and a long history of prize-winning contributors, has arguably the highest reputation for news of any American news publication. *The Washington Post*, being based in the city of the national government, is the newspaper which serves the political and diplomatic community, as well as having a long reputation for investigative journalism (with the 'Watergate' case being the most famous example). All four papers, then, are respected news sources, although they have differing relationships with government. All four make much of their adherence to journalistic standards of objectivity, comprehensiveness, and the pursuit of news. All four would certainly deny the influence of ideological forces.

But whether they like it or not, journalists are not simply reporters – that is, people who convey information. They are teachers, preachers, and ideologists: they tell us how to see and understand the world.[3]

Our task is to trace the lines of such 'seeing and understanding.'

The Berlin Wall

We shall look at the coverage of the opening of the Berlin Wall in November 1989. This followed a series of dramatic political changes in Eastern Europe during 1989, as Communist governments gave up power following President Gorbachev's policy of *perestroika* (reform) in the Soviet Union. East Germany's Stalinist leader Erich Honecker was replaced by the reformist Egon Krenz in October, and in the following weeks pressure mounted on his government to open East Germany's borders as thousands of demonstrators took to the streets in cities such as East Berlin, Leipzig and Dresden. The borders were opened on the evening of Thursday, 9 November, with the most spectacular scenes occurring in Berlin as thousands of East Germans crossed the Berlin Wall to visit the Western sector of the city. Constructed in August 1961, the wall had long been a symbol of the cold war, seeming to make manifest Churchill's famous reference in a 1946 speech to an 'iron curtain' falling across Europe. Its opening was thus an event with a particularly potent symbolic charge.

The pattern of coverage

From one point of view, this was an ideal news item. It was part of a long-running and continuously developing story (the changes in Eastern Europe) but combined with a major element of surprise (the opening of the border, although called for by many people, was completely unexpected). Both of these factors have been shown to be important ingredients in studies of 'news values', that is, the criteria which journalists and news editors use in selecting which items are to be written about and published.[4] In addition, it was highly pictorial, as was clear in the television coverage showing crowds of people rejoicing against a background of such famous buildings as the Brandenburg Gate. From another point of view, it was not such an ideal story. The timing of this unexpected event was unfortunate for the British papers. The first announcement was made shortly before 7 p.m. with the first border crossings taking place at about 9.30 p.m. This was shortly before the London newspapers would be going to press, and they therefore had very little time to reconstruct their newspapers to take account of this major event. The American newspapers were luckier. The transatlantic time difference (7 p.m. in Berlin was 1 p.m. by Eastern Standard Time) meant that for them the events were occurring during the afternoon, rather than the evening, and so their reporting was able to follow the story up until about 3 a.m. giving much more time for developing their coverage.

The story was clearly a major one and in all four papers it covers more than half the front page, including the main headline, although it is interesting to note that none of the four was prepared to devote the entire front page to it. The development and continuation of this coverage takes place inside on the recognized pages for international news (p. 8 in *The Times* and *The Independent*, pp. A14–16 in *The New York Times*, and pp. A37–42 in *The Washington Post*). Three of the papers (the exception is *The Independent*) also have opinion articles on the story (pp. 16 and 17 in *The Times*, p. A36 in *The New York Times*, and p. A26 in *The Washington Post*). The amount of coverage reflects the importance given to the event. This is not a self-evident statement – it would be quite possible for a major story to be treated succinctly and to cover a smaller amount of space than lesser stories. Despite this, newspapers regard size of coverage as one of the prime indicators of importance, along with prominence. Size cannot, however, be judged simply on the basis of page numbers. The two London papers are broadsheets, and so their page is twice the size of the tabloid American papers. In addition, some of the space is taken up by advertising. In *The Washington Post*, for example, two of the pages (A37–8) contain half-page display advertisements. Also, the overall size of the paper must be taken into account – on 10 November 1989 *The Times* had 48 pages, *The Independent* 32, *The New York Times* 38 in its main section (and another 86 in separately numbered specialist sections), and *The Washington Post* a main sequence of 46 (with another 72 in specialist sections). If all these factors are taken into account, it will be seen that the importance of the event, as measured by the space devoted to it, does not vary widely across the four papers. In *The Times* and *The Independent* the coverage is about 5% of the newspaper space, in *The New York Times* it is about 10% of the main section but about 3% of the whole paper, and in *The Washington Post* it is about 8% of the main section, and again about 3% of the whole paper. Given the possible range of sizes (for example, from a half-page article taking up just 0.5% of the newspaper, to a ten-page spread taking up 10% of the whole issue), the difference between 3% and 5% is not great.

This gives the editors the problem of how to fill the space, especially when the event itself can be described fairly briefly. For the London newspapers this was a particular problem since the timing gave them less scope for developing the story. As a result *The Independent*, for example, included several paragraphs from a 1961 speech by the then Russian leader, Nikita Kruschev, and from a

1963 speech by President John Kennedy. There was also a shortage of pictures available at this early stage in the reporting. Three of the papers under consideration had exactly the same photograph (from a French news agency) on their front page, of people on top of the wall. The exception was *The Independent* which made do with an old picture of the wall as it used to be, under heavy guard. Illustrations on inside pages were also limited, with all four papers using historic photographs of events such as President Kennedy speaking at the wall in 1963. The American papers were able to get pictures of celebrating Berliners, although the night-time photographs were not very informative.

It will be obvious even from this outline description of the pattern of news coverage that the four papers structure their accounts in broadly similar ways. A dramatic headline opens the story, followed by the main description of events. This is developed into a number of sub-stories concerning history, personal reaction and international political reaction. Opinion articles (such as editorials) form a further development. The story is then structured as a set of variations on a fairly simple theme. This occurs within two larger structures. One is the overall make-up of the newspaper, which carefully situates the Berlin story as simply one among many others (thus reasserting the newspapers' claims to report all the important news). This is clear from the front page design in which other stories fight for our attention, but also from the categorization of the Berlin item as international news, thereby putting it in its place within the second structure, the newspapers' hierarchy of events. Beyond that a third structure can be discerned – that of the continuously developing story not only of Eastern Europe, but of post-war world history. The reporting thus becomes *overdetermined* – it is affected by its position in several different structures, making a disordered world orderly and merging the chaotic events of history into a meaningful pattern of experience. The similarities in reporting, then, included structure as well as length and illustrative material.

The content itself fell into four categories – description of the events in Berlin, quotations from Berliners at the scene of events, reactions from other countries, and historical contextualizations. It is worth noting right away that only the first of these four categories falls completely under the traditional journalist's description of his or her task, that is, the objective investigation and description of significant events. The other three categories are all embellishments of one kind or another, moving away from objectivity into the realm of opinion.

The second category – the Berliners' own statements – may at first seem to add important detail to the reporting, as well as allowing a variety of voices to reach the newspaper page. However, these quotations are often anonymous ('a student said that . . .') or, if a name is given, it is, in effect, meaningless since unknown to the reader and not given enough context. When we add to this that the comments quoted are limited to the expression of emotion or immediate intention, it will be seen that the quotations are used merely to add colour and life to the reporting. The following example from *The Washington Post* is typical.

> 'I'm just going over to have a look', one excited man said. Another said: 'My wife is at home crying her eyes out because she has to look after the kids and can't come'.[5]

Some are even less informative, such as this quotation in *The New York Times*.

> 'I can't describe it,' a young woman said with tears in her eyes.[6]

It need hardly be said that such quotations are also highly selective – three or four statements from people in a situation of sudden change are given as representative of the nation at large.

The third category is largely devoted to reporting politicians' statements, that is, their opinions, and it is safe to assume that the reporters did not have to go out of their way to persuade politicians to speak to them. In the contrast between (in the journalists' view) the powerful – the recognized politicans who are named and whose opinion is sought out – and the powerless – the ordinary people swept along by events, often quoted anonymously, and usually only asked for their emotional reactions – there is a clear assertion of hierarchy between the élite and the ordinary, between the people who matter and those who do not. The structures of power are reflected and supported by the structures of reporting.

The historical approach

The fourth category of content – historical contextualization – has a role in news reporting that cannot easily be overestimated. Daniel Hallin explains this as follows.

> Journalists not only tell us where a particular event took place, they also tell us where we are in a more general and much more important sense.[7]

John Fiske has expressed a similar thought.

> They tell the story of the past not only to make sense of the present, but to make common sense of the present.[8]

As already noted in an earlier chapter, common sense is a standard marker of ideology at work. Such historical sense-making is well illustrated in the Berlin Wall reporting. It is treated as the end of a story which has structured our lives for some time. The American papers tend to see 1961, when the wall was built, as the start of the story and, in giving its history, once again use the élite/ordinary opposition. Politicians' visits and speeches are noted (in particular Kennedy's 'Ich bin ein Berliner' speech) and the ingenuity of attempts to cross the wall are celebrated. The British papers, while also recounting this history, start the story earlier with Winston Churchill's 'iron curtain' speech in 1946. *The Times* even includes a direct quotation from a 1946 issue of the newspaper, including a reproduced headline.

Some extracts will give the flavour of this historicizing, beginning with a very clear example from *The Times*.

> Herr Günter Schabowski, the Politburo member responsible for the media, said that the new ruling came into effect immediately — 43 years after Winston Churchill proclaimed, in a speech in Fulton, Missouri, that an 'iron curtain' had descended across Europe.[9]

The next example sets up a dramatic contrast with the events of 1961.

> At Checkpoint Charlie, where Allied and Soviet tanks were locked in a tense face-off while the Berlin wall was being erected in August 1961, lines of cars and people began to file across the border by late evening. (*The New York Times*)[10]

Here the situation is set up as the reverse image of the building of the wall. Another example sets the historical context of oppression, writing the story as a traditional narrative of liberation.

> East Germany last night decided to throw open the Berlin Wall and its heavily fortified 'iron curtain' border and let its unhappy people go. (*The Independent*)[11]

(Interestingly this was changed in later editions to omit the 'unhappy people' reference). Meanwhile *The Washington Post*, although emphasizing a 1961 start to the story in much of its reporting, made sure that the longer historical view was not forgotten.

> Communist East Germany today opened its borders to the West, including the Berlin Wall, announcing that its citizens could travel or emigrate freely, in the most stunning step since World War II toward ending the East-West division of Europe.[12]

Sometimes the historical narrative merges with the well-worn narratives of popular culture.

It was a monument to political control, a scene of gunfire and drama and tragedy, the stuff of spy novels and a physical and psychic barrier that divided Berlin, Germany and Europe. For 28 years, the Berlin wall has been the foremost symbol of cold war and East-West confrontation. (*The New York Times*)[13]

Even more significant is the worry felt when the historical context seems to be an inadequate explanation. Thus the editorial in *The Times* talks about 'the rapid and bewildering sequence of events' and expresses concern that 'these events are plainly no longer part of any disciplined or coherent design'.[14] A feeling comes across here of events being made to fit historical patterns only with difficulty. The simplicities of cold war oppositions begin to seem too limited, lacking explanatory power as East European governments respond to popular demonstrations. This is expressed in *The Independent* by a full page heading which states 'As East German borders open, the world ponders a future in which the Wall has lost its meaning'.[15] The ideological certainty which the Wall symbolized is suddenly found to be inadequate and this change gains expression in the newspapers.

The problem with these contextualizations is not that they are 'wrong': within a particular ideological schema they cannot easily be disproved, and newspapers are clearly expected to provide some kind of explanation. The problem is that they are stated as unquestioned absolutes and thus close down alternative interpretations of events, attempting to leave the reader firmly placed within, and subjected to, an ideological framework. Particular historical interpretations are presented in the same way as 'objective fact'. This is most obvious above in *The Washington Post's* confident assertion of the opening of the wall as 'the most stunning step' in East-West relations since 1945, presented not as historical opinion but in the same manner as neutral description. In addition to this, the historical writing tends to overwhelm the reporting of the event itself, which becomes instant history, wrapped up neatly for general consumption with uncertainties and complexities relegated to the background. Thus the event is inserted into one particular discourse, one particular way of describing and explaining it, and other discourses are actively discouraged. As John Fiske has written, 'news discourse has to repress these discursive alternatives, it tries to censor out the unrealized discursive potential of events'.[16]

The personal approach

The content, then, can be categorized fairly easily, but equally important are the techniques used to convey this material to us.

Foremost amongst these is the personalizing of events, which leads to the constant asserting of human will and choice over broader determinants of change, and provides hooks for the reader's desire to identify with characters. Individualism – a mainstay of capitalist ideology in its denial of the relevance of classs, gender and race – becomes a determining force. This particular story was not by its nature concerned with individuals. Mass pressure on a government had led to a collective decision being made, and that decision had led to further mass action as the wall was breached. It would be quite possible to give a description of these happenings without reference to any specific person. However, the journalists' need to humanize the story led to its being transformed into an account of individual actions.

This personalization can be seen to be working in various ways. The East German government's decision is personalized by referring either to Egon Krenz, the government leader at the time, or to Gunter Schabowski, who made the public announcement. The description of the events at the wall itself very quickly becomes the account of individual reactions. And, as already noted, the reactions of foreign governments become personalized as the reactions of well-known politicians, such as Helmut Kohl in West Germany, Mikhail Gorbachev in the Soviet Union and George Bush in the United States. It is worth noting that the journalists' need for personal reactions forced these politicians into making statements at an early stage in the development of the event, before they or their colleagues were fully aware of even the most immediate consequences. Many of these statements were, to say the least, unremarkable. President Bush was quoted as describing the event as a 'dramatic happening for East Germany and, of course, for freedom'.[17]

Another aspect of the personalizing of the story is the use of reporters' names. In all four papers the main stories are given authors (for example, 'East Berliners Explore Land Long Forbidden, by Ferdinand Protzman, Special to The New York Times',[18] 'East Germans Start to Travel Freely as 28-year Barrier Falls, from Patricia Clough in East Berlin'[19]). Such 'authorization' is not essential in newspapers, indeed many stories will be anonymous or simply give a general source such as a news agency ('From Reuters') or a description of a role ('From our Berlin correspondent'). In such a context, giving a named author has its own meaning. It is partly an assertion of authenticity ('I, the named writer, was there and saw it with my own eyes') – given added weight by saying where the journalist is reporting from. It is also, however, an assertion of authority ('I, the named writer, am an important enough journalist to get my name in the paper and therefore my words carry weight'). This process is at its most blatant on the front page of *The Independent*, which carries an article in which 'Neal Ascherson reflects on a night that changed the European cosmos'.[20] Thus the value placed on the individual is carried over into the seemingly objective world of factual reporting.

Positioning the reader

Consideration of the techniques used to present the story brings us on to the question of how the reader is positioned. As we saw in chapter 2, ideology works to position us in a particular way, so we should be able to trace this process in the text. The mode of address, which works to make ideological subjects of us, can be seen in these newspapers in several forms. Firstly, assumptions are made about our interests. The treatment of the event as a major story assumes that we, the readers, will share that opinion. The reports are not written in order to convince us that it is a major event, but rather this is the unstated premise – unstated because the newspaper assumes there is no need to state it. That it is an assumption can be illustrated by what happens when the assumption of importance is not shared. When the black South African leader Nelson Mandela was released from prison on 11 February 1990, BBC Television interrupted a popular programme (*The Antiques Roadshow*) to show live coverage of the event. This programme, in which members of the public submit what they believe may be valuable objects in their possession to the scrutiny of a panel of experts for identification and valuation, is clearly aimed at a predominantly well-off, middle-class and (at least) middle-aged audience. This is precisely the social group which is least likely to be sympathetic to Mandela. It was not surprising then that this interruption resulted in many people writing and phoning their complaints to the BBC. Many of the complainants did not simply object to the interruption of the programme, but claimed that the release of Mandela was not really important and was being blown out of all proportion by the media. Ideologically this can be seen as a rejection of the assumption of importance which any news story treated as major implies.

Another technique for positioning the audience is the way in which the reporter becomes a stand-in for the reader. The eye-witness account, and the emotional reaction from participants, both much loved by news editors in all the mass media, can be seen as ways of positioning the audience within, or at least beside, the news event. By standing in for us, the reporter is able to make it seem that the interviewees are speaking directly to the audience. On the front page of *The Times* an East Berlin student is quoted as saying, 'It is as if our country has finally opened its eyes to reality'.[21] This gives us a personal reaction at the scene, as though the student were speaking directly to us. The 'reality' referred to is, of course, an ideological construction which the readers of the newspaper are presumed to share, thus confirming the process of putting the readers into a conversation with the witnesses. The highly selective nature of the quote (Was this student typical? What else did he say? Was he in an emotional state when he said it? Was the quote chosen simply because it echoed the reporter's own response?) is hidden by the seeming authenticity of direct conversation.

Conclusion

As a concluding note it is appropriate to mention the role of professional ideologies. A professional (or occupational) ideology is a variant of the broader ideologies of class, gender and nationality, and works to defend a particular occupation as something valuable, unique and requiring special skills (and thus special rewards). Journalists' professional ideology includes the commitments to objectivity and investigation mentioned earlier. It also, however, includes other more specific elements which are not echoed in the broader ideology. One of these is an exaggerated respect for time (well documented in Philip Schlesinger's study of BBC journalistic practices in the early 1970s)[22] which can lead to its own particular distortions of reporting. In the case in hand, the need to fill a specific amount of the newspaper (reflecting the event's perceived importance) by a specific time (set by production practices rather than by any imperative in the news itself) results in an exaggeration of the historical contextualization, since this is the one aspect of the coverage which can be developed easily without leaving the newspaper office. *The Independent*'s long quotes from historic speeches are merely the most obvious examples of this. As always, such ideological elements work to preserve the status quo and to reproduce the conditions of their own existence. Thus the common ideological practice of narrating a history and personalizing events is used not just in aid of a dominant ideology but also in defence of the narrower concerns of a professional ideology – that of journalists. The result is an event rendered meaningful by its insertion into an ideological structure – a structure which is remarkably consistent across four different newspapers in two countries.

6 Narrating the championship

So far we have been concerned primarily with the use of written language. We will now move beyond this by turning to an event and the texts which circulate around it, in order to develop the complexity of the analysis. The event chosen is an international sporting occasion. Sport is quite clearly an important part of the culture of modern societies. It is the arena in which conflicts for both the individual and the nation can be played out symbolically. It involves ideas of human nature, nationality and gender as well as assumptions about achievement, conflict and skill. Sport is one of the few areas in which the myth that anyone can be a success does actually have some small particle of truth – at least in those sports which do not involve expensive equipment. It is also, of course, a multi-million pound international business, and one which regularly occupies a substantial amount of space in newspapers and on television, quite apart from the large numbers of people who attend sporting events as spectators.

It should be stressed that we are concerned here with the analysis of a specific event and some of the textual material associated with it. We are not concerned with the broader question of the ideological function of sport in general – that is, we are concerned with one event, not with the overall institution of sport in modern societies. Reading on this broader issue can be found, most comprehensively, in John Hargreaves's *Sport, Power and Culture*. There, Hargreaves develops the thesis that sport has a hegemonic funcion in modern society. Since their restructuring in Britain in the mid-Victorian period, the major sports have worked as a means of incorporating elements of the working class within the overall structures of society, and as a means of providing 'divisive non-class identities'.[1]

> Sports have contributed to bourgeois hegemony in two different but nevertheless related ways: on the one hand by helping to fragment the working class in particular, as well as subordinate groups in general; and on the other hand, by reconstituting them within a unified social formation under bourgeois hegemony. On the whole, sports unify dominant groups and supporting classes, while disorganizing and fragmenting subordinate ones.[2]

This is not to deny the undoubted pleasures and satisfactions which involvement in sport gives to many people. Indeed the incorporation of sport into contemporary consumer culture is based on the promise of satisfaction of a wide range of needs concerning the body. As Hargreaves notes, sport, which has become in this age perhaps the means of body expression *par excellence*, feeds such needs with rewarding experiences of its own — of fitness, movement, energy, force, speed, play, competition and dramatic, ritualized activity.[3]

The above makes clear how complex may be the pleasures of such a seemingly straightforward activity as sport and suggests that its ideological role may also be more complicated than it might appear to be (as is evident also from more recent writing on the subject[4]).

Since our task here is to demonstrate methods of ideological analysis, we will concentrate on just one event — the British Open Golf Championship. Writing on sport has tended to concentrate on the mass spectator sports, such as football. By choosing golf we are choosing one with a large international following but which presents problems of analysis not present in the compact and intensive conflicts of stadium sports.

The event

The 118th British Open Golf Championship took place between Thursday 20 and Sunday 23 July 1989. The setting was the Royal Troon Golf Course in Ayrshire on the west coast of Scotland. It was a commercial event attracting golfers from all round the world. Of the 156 who took part, aiming for some of the £750,000 of prize money, 71 came from the British Isles, 46 from the United States, 11 from Australia and 7 from South Africa. Nine other countries were represented in the line-up (Argentina, Denmark, Fiji, France, Japan, Spain, Sweden, West Germany, and Zimbabwe) with between one and five players each. Ten of the entrants were amateurs, the rest professionals. The British Open is regarded as the premier British golf competition. It is structured as a four-day event. On each of the first two days, the competitors play 18 holes each, teeing off in threes. For the third and fourth days, the number of players is halved, being limited to the first 70 and any who had an equal score with the 70th. On this occasion a total of 80 was left for the last two days. By the end of the fourth round on Sunday, three players (Mark Calcavecchia, Wayne Grady, and Greg Norman) tied for first place and so they teed off together for a deciding round of four holes (the 1st, 2nd, 17th and 18th). This finally produced a clear winner (Calcavecchia) on Sunday evening. Thus the event started with the first players beginning at 7.15 a.m. on Thursday, and ended at about 7.10 p.m. on Sunday. On each day substantial numbers of spectators attended (television commentator Harry Carpenter refers to 35,000 turning up to watch the third day's play on Saturday). There was also a pattern of daily live television coverage, mostly on the BBC2 channel, with summaries of the day's highlights in a 40 or 45 minute programme shown late in the evening.

Before considering the structure of this event, an important point needs to be mentioned. Despite being called the 'Open' championship it is an event for men only. There is a separate women's championship. The reason cited for keeping the two championships separate is that strength can play an important part in golf, and men are conventionally thought to be stronger than women. However, this does not explain the fact that the male championship is seen as the top event, rather than as equal to the women's event. It is also worth noting that other formats could be used. Men and women could take part in the same event but be awarded separate prizes (one title for best man and one for best woman), or the two championships could be held together, giving the women as much publicity as the men, or indeed men and women could compete against each other – some women are clearly stronger than the average man, and in a sport like golf skill can sometimes overcome the advantage of strength. Instead of these options, however, golf remains a male-dominated sport – at least as far as the major events are concerned. If, as devotees of sports usually claim, the enjoyment of spectating comes from the display of skill and determination, then there is no reason for such male orientation. In an interesting essay, Eric Dunning has suggested that sports are essentially concerned with masculinity and male identity.[5] He suggests that the origin of many sports lies in pre-industrial games of violence, which, apart from allowing aggression to take place in a broadly acceptable form, also privileged male participation, due to the need for strength and aggressiveness. Dunning's argument is strongest when dealing with such team games as football and rugby, but it may also go some way to explaining male domination of other sports, even ones as non-violent as golf (and, after all, golf is essentially concerned with the violent – if skilful – manipulation of a club). It would also help to explain the irrational way in which many men tend to resist sharing sports with women. The ideology of gender is here playing an important role.

Another general point to make is that golf can be played in various ways, unlike team games such as football. It is quite possible to play it alone, simply getting pleasure from the attempt to keep one's score as low as possible. On the other hand, it can be played with as large a number as a golf course can take. The number of rounds is variable, with the basic unit of eighteen holes capable of any number of multiplications (and even that is not sacrosanct, as the four-hole play-off in this championship showed). Major competitions usually take place over several days. The game can also be structured either as *match-play*, in which the winner is the one who wins the most individual holes, or as *stroke-play*, in which the winner is the one with the lowest total score of shots. In addition, it must be emphasized that golf is not a natural spectator's game. Unlike most team games which are played in a restricted arena allowing all the audience to see all the play, golf gives the spectator the choice of remaining at one position on the course and therefore seeing all the players but only at that one point, or following round one small group of players, thus seeing their play over the whole course but missing that of all the other competitors.

The British Open, like all commercially organized sports, is designed with two overlapping aims in mind – to make the competition a challenge for the entrants, and to make it exciting for the spectators. Thus the four-day structure (with two days at a weekend) makes it more likely that spectators will be able to watch the whole event than it would be if it was staged over, for example, eight days. It also makes it a manageable event for entrants, while lessening the advantages which the weather can provide for lucky players in a one-day open-air event. (Even in the four-day event the weather had a role to play, when rain fell during the second day, getting worse as the day wore on, thus favouring those competitors who had started earliest). Similarly the decision to send competitors round the course in groups of three not only made the game more pleasurable for them, but also provided spectators with, as it were, mini-competitions at every hole. Perhaps more important, however, is the effect of cutting out half the field after the first two days. This provides a real sense of progress and rivalry which helps to bring the competition to a climax. In this particular event, the play-off among the three leaders after the fourth round added the excitement of a final shoot-out. It would have been quite possible to end the competition with joint winners splitting the prize money. (And, in fact, although the eventual winner had the largest prize, the two others who were involved in the play-off received the same prize, regardless of who was second and who was third). The fight to a single winner, however, provides players and spectators with a more satisfying conclusion, in effect giving a stronger closure to the event.

The narrativization process

The question then arises as to the ideological significance of these factors. This is best demonstrated by noting how the golfing event is *narrativized*, that is, it is treated as the performance of a story. The authors of *Key Concepts in Communication* describe narrative as 'the devices, strategies and conventions governing the organization of a story (fictional or factual) into a sequence' and suggest that it can be analysed into two main categories.[6] The first is *plot* – the events of the narrative and the order in which they occur. The second is *narration* – the way in which the plot is told, or related. Plots involve characters, actions and causal relations (without causality the plot becomes a random collection of unexplained and unconnected events). Narration puts these elements into a framework addressed to an audience. We have already (in the previous chapter) seen a version of this process taking place in news reporting as the newspaper accounts are structured like a story and the news event is made to fit into historical narratives. By arguing that the golf championship is narrativized, we are suggesting that the event itself is made to conform to the conventions of stories and storytelling. The event becomes charged with particular meanings as it is made to accommodate elements from other mythic narratives. Fredric Jameson, in the subtitle to *The Political Unconscious*, talks of 'narrative as a socially symbolic act'.[7] Thus to narrativize a sporting event is to give it a symbolic social value – that is, an ideological meaning. This process of narrativization can be seen as taking place in two stages. First, there is the organization of the event itself. Second, there is the discourse set up around the event, that is, the secondary texts which describe and discuss the event, guiding the audience's reactions. These are most obviously the newspaper and television commentaries.

The principal way in which the organization of the event leads to narrativization is in its structuring. This gives the event a beginning (the first round with no scores on the board – its blankness becomes the agenda), a middle (the winnowing out of the field and the appearance of likely winners from a series of minor conflicts) and an end (the single victor who has overcome all the obstacles and resolved the enigma of the blank score board). This structure, combined with the grouping of competitors into threes as they set off round the course, ensures the emergence of 'characters' (The Winner, The Unlucky Loser, The Failed Old-Timer, The Best Young Challenger, The Dark Horse, etc.). Such characterization owes more to fiction than to sport. The organization of spectators (notably the grandstand set up by the final green) functions to highlight certain aspects of the game, concentrating attention on those moments when victory and defeat are most clearly demonstrated. This process of narrativization moves the emphasis away from the skill involved in the game to the elements of conflict and their resolution. The symbolic element enters when the game is interpreted according to abstract notions of human nature, which make links to other manifestations of these same values. Thus the game becomes a metaphor for life in general. It becomes one version of the 'grand narrative' of our society, the myth of ideology which explains human nature and human society. It is the myth in which individual effort is rewarded by a supreme accolade, and all background to the contest is interpreted as the histories of individual heroes. Social origins and economic context are made irrelevant as personal struggle and determination fight to overcome every obstacle.

The newspaper commentary

The most obvious contribution of media coverage to the narrativization process, other than the emphasizing of the structure of the event, is in the creation of heroes. Newspaper commentary, for example, was almost entirely founded on the celebration of (or, in some cases in which heroes became tragic heroes, the commiseration with) famous individuals. The ultimate winner, Mark Calcavecchia, was not particularly famous (that is, had not already been prominently featured as a hero) and there was very little comment about him, even in the British Sunday morning papers (by which time he was lying in fourth place, only three strokes behind the leader, and thus ideally placed for the final round). Instead, commentary focused on heroes of earlier events, such as Tom Watson, Greg Norman and Nick Faldo. Even lesser-known names whose lives could be linked to common story patterns received more coverage. David Feherty, who, when younger, had had to choose between a career as an opera singer and as a professional golfer, is an example. The making of such a choice and his subsequent success (he ended the competition as the highest-placed player from the British Isles) becomes a sign of his heroic status. As in many traditional stories, the hero is confirmed when he correctly chooses between alternatives. Items which appeared in newspapers about individual golfers invariably set their current achievement in the context of their professional golfing careers, thus referring to other narratives. Their task is defined in story-telling terms, with their professional lives being treated as epic journeys through a land of obstacles. Three examples from different newspapers will indicate how this works.

The first is by Ken Jones in *The Independent*, writing about Tom Watson.

> Watson does not flinch from the truth, admitting to frailties, living with the possibility that he will never again enjoy the status of a man to be feared on the golf course, not forgotten but naggingly an outsider when the odds are drawn up.
>
> Now there is a calmness, as though he has finally come to terms with the passing of time, his slump rationalised so that he can speak of patience as a great virtue.[8]

Here Watson is spoken of as a hero from the past who has achieved a mature serenity after the self-knowledge brought on by earlier defeats, rather like a character from a film (such as an ageing detective in a crime story). The second example is from John Samuel, writing in *The Guardian*.

> Seve Ballesteros, 10 shots behind the leader, outrageously turned spokesman last night for the cluster who lie in ambush on the bottom half of the leader board. 'I will be playing early tomorrow morning. If I have nice weather and a low score, and if the weather starts blowing in the afternoon, who knows, I have a chance', he said. And smiled. Ballesteros, of course, is the patron saint of redeemed lost causes. He was as far behind at Turnberry and shot a last-round 64 which threatened everyone except Greg Norman for an ultimate sixth place.[9]

Reference to ambushes, lost causes, and dramatic finishes make the narrativization fairly obvious here. The third example is from Hugh McIlvanney writing about Greg Norman in *The Observer* (in an article significantly entitled 'Norman's Major Mission').

> When a golfer as talented as Greg Norman has taken only one of the game's great titles by the age of 34, every subsequent major championship that goes to somebody else will seem to point at him in accusation.
>
> As Norman enters the last round of the 118th Open at Royal Troon today, these long-term pressures give no evidence of contaminating the amiable, cavalier optimism golf's happiest multi-millionaire has always brought to the course. But among his warmest admirers the perennial surge of expectation is noticeably infected by anxiety. They worry over the depressing possibility that, a decade on, Greg Norman's career will still be without the mile-stones of triumph in the majors to let posterity know the true, outrageous measure of his gifts.[10]

Here the hero's lack of fit with his tragic role (his cheerfulness, his wealth) is circumvented by passing the tragic awareness on to his followers, thus making his own position seem even more tragic.

Such writing about sport is so standard that it may seem odd to regard it as anything other than a harmless indulgence, perhaps even the commonsense way. How else should we write about the Open Golf Championship if not in terms of individual struggle? The answer is that there are many ways of writing a story and if one seems obvious then that is only because our expectations have been shaped in that way. In other words, ideology leads us to make judgments about what is 'commonsense'.

The television commentary

The most revealing television coverage is not the daytime live broadcasting but the selected and edited highlights broadcast in the late evening.[11] The concentration of a full day's play into 45 minutes performs the same act as is seen in newspaper coverage – attitudes to the event are underlined in the process of selection. The most obvious way in which this works is to emphasize the play of the known players, those who have already featured as heroes in other championship narratives. The only times lesser-known or virtually unknown players are shown is when they temporarily go into the lead. Thus of the 156 entrants, only 18 are shown in the first day's highlights, and several of these only very briefly. The concentration is on the well-known players such as Nick Faldo, Seve Ballesteros, and Tom Watson. This becomes very obvious when the first day's highlights begin with the following commentary.

> Play started here at a quarter past seven this morning and at ten o'clock Nick Faldo walked on to the first tee – US Masters Champion, Open Champion two years ago at Muirfield, and one of the pre-championship favourites.

The first two and three-quarter hours of play are simply passed over. Even by the third day's play, after the field has been cut down to the 80 best players, only 13 are shown in the evening.

The degree of selection is far greater than just this, however. There is a very heavy concentration on showing the last few holes – the ones at which the leadership of the competition is confirmed. On the Thursday highlights, the last two holes (the 17th and 18th) are shown most frequently, with the 15th and 16th not far behind. Of the 14 other holes, action is shown at only four. On the Friday night, the last three holes are the most popular, with the 14th and 15th slightly less so, and only five others being shown, three of them very briefly. There is nothing obvious about this coverage. If the aim of the selection is to show the most skilful play, then one would expect a much wider range of players and of holes. It is interesting to note that the eventual winner, Mark Calcavecchia, is not shown at all on the Thursday highlights, and only briefly on Friday at the 17th green. As already noted, he had not featured in Britain as a sporting hero and the newspapers also ignored him until late on in the competition.

Another feature of the television coverage is its concentration on the greens, that is, on the moments at which holes are won and lost – despite the fact that this is a stroke-play, not a match-play, championship. There is clearly a visual element at work here. The hitting of the ball, the ball's movement, and its final position are all easily followed on the green, as they cannot be when, for example, driving off the tee, in which little more than the hitting can be clearly shown. In addition, cameras can be placed at the optimum position, whereas when golfers are on the fairway between the tee and the green it is difficult to predict precisely where the best camera position will be. Thus there are strong practical considerations for the emphasis on the greens. However, such considerations should not blind us to two points. The first is that these 'practical' consider- ations are themselves based on assumptions about what makes 'good television' – that is, assumptions about what audiences like to watch. They are thus not ideologically innocent but rather are them- selves indicators of widely held values. The second point to remem- ber is that, regardless of the reasons for such choices, the effects (the television coverage as it is broadcast) will have a particular structure and a particular range of meanings which will be delivered to the viewers. It should be clear from this how televisual style can have ideological determinations.

The television coverage, then, takes the process of concentration on heroic conflict a degree further, with its emphasis on known heroes, and the moments when the leadership of the contest is changing or under threat. Skill is simply treated as an added bonus, a by-product of watching the famous players. The commentary, as might be expected, helps this process and makes the narrativization clear (although it is not as blatant as that in the newspapers). At the end of the first day's play, the BBC commentator, Harry Carpenter, had this to say about the first round leader, Wayne Stephens.

> Well, let me now add my congratulations to young Wayne Stephens – 28 years old, born in Jersey, the unknown player who came out and showed the world's greatest players the way round Royal Troon.

Stephens is thus firmly placed as a character in this narrative. Simi- larly the older players are located in the story.

> Now, what about some of these former Open Champions playing here this week? Let's see how they got on today.

It is at the end, however, that the process is most apparent. A commentator, talking of Greg Norman during the final play-off, refers to 'that fateful evening in Augusta just a few years ago' when another championship was lost. Of Calcavecchia, despite the earlier ignoring of him, it is said at the end, 'So he came, he saw, he conquered'.[12] A modern narrator quotes from an ancient one in this act of narrative closure.

Conclusion

The narrativization process should now be clear. The event and the commentaries surrounding it are treated as stories to be related. These stories promote traditional values and convert actual people into quasi-fictional characters. The championship is thus able to participate in what Hargreaves terms sport's hegemonic role, through its ideological translation. A seemingly open sport becomes a vehicle for hegemonically implicated values. Golfing skill becomes of secondary importance as the game becomes an epic of heroic conflict, with individuals battling each other, seeming to prove that 'it's only commonsense', that this is the way things are. Just as in traditional societies epic stories are used to pass on the culture's values, so in modern societies sporting events are one of the means by which a similar function is performed.

7 Chatting to the nation

Central to any study of contemporary culture must be the examination of television output. It forms the central spine of our information-based society – it is our main source of news, whether local or foreign, our source of drama, whether real or fictional, and our source of knowledge about our culture, whether past or present. Our sense of ourselves is mediated in significant ways by our interaction with the television set. To get some idea of the ideological significance of this medium, we will analyse an example of popular prime-time programming.[1] Studies of various types of programming are already available.[2] However, one type of programme which has not, so far, attracted much attention is the talk show (or 'chat show'). This is odd, for the show's format seems to reflect the overall structure of television output – a popular television personality provides a friendly framework within which a series of guests appear. Just as a television station fits very different kinds of programme into a structure of continuity, so the talk show fits a series of different speakers into a familiar and stable pattern.

Their reflection of television structure does not explain the popularity of talk shows. To do so, other factors must be considered. To account for their popularity with the programmers, we need only consider how cheap they are to make. A minimal, unchanging set, the simplest of television techniques, guests who are usually more than willing to gain the publicity, and an assured audience attracted partly by the personality of the host – financially it is a programme-maker's dream, with the only unusually high cost being the host's salary (and, since the programme seems to depend so completely on the host, such salaries can be extremely high).

From the audience's point of view, their popularity is related to several factors, apart from the host's personality. The indulgence of voyeurism is a major factor, most obvious in American shows such as those of Phil Donohue and Oprah Winfrey, in which sex is a constant topic, but present in all types of chat show, even if it is partially suppressed (as we shall see later). Such programmes are usually shown live and this adds to the viewer's enjoyment – an element of risk is added to the familiar structure. The best talk show hosts go out of their way to emphasize this so that the audience is constantly reminded that a live show is being watched, with the implication that they are eavesdropping on a private conversation. The host, of course, has a more personal reason for emphasizing the live element. In the professional ideology of broadcasters, live television has an important place.[3] The presenter who can cope with a live discussion programme can consider him or herself to be at the top of the professional broadcaster's tree. (Interestingly, this aspect becomes explicit in the third of the three programmes looked at below when one of the guests – himself a television personality – praises the host for coping with a well-publicized last-minute change of guest on the Wednesday programme). This professional ideology is important as a way of letting the presenter come to terms with the realities of contemporary television. Dominated by complex technologies (which can alter the very image of the presenter) she or he is, in fact, just one element in the programme. By emphasizing the ability to cope with live programming, the presenter puts the emphasis back onto him or herself. This ideology has its roots in the early days of television broadcasting when, as the profession of television performer was being defined, all output, even drama, was live.

It is tempting to divide talk shows into two kinds – those in which the guests are ordinary people and those in which they are celebrities. However, although there are real differences between these two styles, the essential format is the same. In addition, many talk shows will straddle both categories, even if they remain based in one.

Wogan

The specific example to be analysed here is the show that, in the late eighties, was one of the most popular talk shows on British television – *Wogan*. The host, Terry Wogan, had long been established as a broadcasting personality before his talk show began. Born in Limerick in the Irish Republic, Wogan has played to the hilt the stereotype of the genial, talkative and slightly naïve Irishman. This role has taken him from his first broadcasting work in his native country to the centre of British broadcasting culture. Marking his status as, in a mild way, an 'outsider' in British society, it has also allowed him to make fun (very gently) of broadcasting conventions, although this was less apparent in his talk show than it had been in his other shows. His early morning radio show (BBC Radio 2, 6.30 a.m.–10 a.m.) began in 1975 and had become extremely popular. He had also been host of a popular television celebrity panel game, *Blankety Blank*, which had been broadcast at a prime slot on Saturday evening since 1982 (and had been a popular weekday programme for some years before that). The success of these two shows had resulted in his being given several awards as 'television personality of the year'. At the end of 1984 he was taken off radio and given a prime-time television talk show, beginning in February

1985. This was part of a much publicized attempt by the BBC (with its new BBC1 programme controller, Michael Grade) to recapture the weekday early evening audience from the rival network of ITV (the other main line of attack was the BBC's new soap opera, *EastEnders*). The BBC's intentions were made clear in an article in their magazine *Radio Times*, to mark the show's start.

> He's aiming to become as much a part of the national psyche in his new role of Early Evening Face as he was when he was the Early Morning Voice.[4]

Wogan went out three times each week, on Monday, Wednesday and Friday, beginning at 7 p.m. and lasting for between 30 and 40 minutes. This timing meant that the programme was aimed at the mass family audience, with the consequence that it would have to provide content that was attractive and interesting, but which would not alienate any major sector of that audience. In ideological terms, we can suggest that the programme's intention was to capture a large audience by confirming and reinforcing the majority audience's view of itself, avoiding minorities (unless they could be treated as eccentric guests) and keeping the content within the bounds of ideological agreement.

As specific examples one week's output will be considered – the shows broadcast on Monday 11 September, Wednesday 13 September and Friday 15 September, 1989.[5] By this time the programme was not as popular as in its earlier days but it was still averaging audiences of over six and a half million.[6] The first step in analysing these shows must be to consider their structure. This stucture is very strong and well-defined, as the following will make clear.

Monday

1. Introduction by Wogan (1.30 min.)
2. First guest – British Olympic athlete Linford Christie (10 min.)
3. Musical interlude – song by Eartha Kitt (3.45 min.)
4. Second guest – singer Eartha Kitt (12 min.)
5. Conclusion by Wogan (0.30 min.)

Wednesday

1. Introduction by Wogan (1.45 min.)
2. First two guests – teenage desert island castaways Martin Popplewell and Rachel Stevens (10.30 min.)
3. Third guest – traveller and explorer Lt.Col. John Blatchford-Snell (8.45 min.)

4. Musical interlude – song by Karyn White (4 min.)
5. Fourth guest – Australian soap opera star Stefan Dennis (8 min.)
6. Very brief conclusion by Wogan

Friday

1. Introduction by Wogan (1.45 min.)
2. First guest – Richard Daley, Mayor of Chicago (12 min.)
3. Musical interlude – song by Roger Christian (3.40 min.)
4. Second guest – British television personality Bruce Forsyth (11 min.)
5. Very brief conclusion by Wogan

The most notable feature of this structure is its unvarying nature. Only very occasionally does *Wogan* depart from it. The only regular form of variation is that sometimes the guests before the musical break stay to join in the conversation with the guests from after the break (as happened in the Wednesday programme above) – a minor variation in an unchanging format. Such a pattern of regularity carries its own message of familiarity and predictability. (This is, of course, the clear intention of the schedulers in placing the programme in an early evening slot.) But its implications go beyond mere familiarity.

Choosing guests and asking questions

Familiarity is reassuring, working by repetition. But within this repetition the programme must try to fit enough variety and novelty to give the audience at least the appearance of something different. The problem for the programme-makers is how to balance this novelty with familiarity. Their answer is to parade a seemingly endless line of different people, suggesting that the programme's content is infinitely variable. However, when we look more closely at who appears, and how they are treated, this claim to endless variety looks less convincing. The guests are usually achievers – they have already had some success, usually in show business, but also in other fields such as sports or (occasionally) politics. Even the two teenagers in the Wednesday programme described above had achieved what is to many people a fantasy dream – being alone for a prolonged length of time on an idyllic Pacific island with a member of the opposite sex. (The fantasy element was emphasized in Wogan's introduction in which he referred to both Robinson Crusoe and *Blue Lagoon*). Also worth noting is the predominance of personalities who are known through television. Even the athlete, Linford Christie, was known primarily through television coverage of his achievements, and characters such as Lt.Col. Blatchford-Snell and Bruce Forsyth were familiar guests on the show (such reappearances are very common on *Wogan*). Thus simply by its selection of guests the programme becomes a celebration of achievement, defined in terms of publicly recognizable success. (The teenagers had already had such public recognition, since before their appearance on *Wogan* there had been stories in the popular press about them).

Such a guest list could, of course, result in a challenging, radical programme, with tough questions on the successes which the guests had achieved. This does not happen on *Wogan*. The questions are designed to allow maximum room for manoeuvre and to elicit no more than comforting 'chat'. The model for this kind of television is not the interview of the investigative journalist, but the domestic conversation with an admired friend. Some examples will make this clear. In the first programme, during the interview with black athlete Linford Christie, two controversial issues appear – drugs and racism. The first issue becomes a joke about the effects of steroids on the male physique. The second issue – race – is referred to by Christie when he comments that when not winning he is described by commentators as 'Jamaican-born Linford Christie' whereas when he is winning the description becomes 'Linford Christie of Britain'. Wogan's response to this is worth quoting.

> That must hurt. Let's hope there won't be any more of it, because everybody's very proud of you and very proud of the team.

With that, the issue of racism is dismissed. The endemic racism implied by Christie's comment is marginalized as Wogan interpellates the audience through his generalizing. It is worth noting that a significant part of the rest of the programme is devoted to the colourful running gear which Christie is well-known for wearing. The potentially explosive issues of drugs and racism get lost in the general chat. Similarly in the Wednesday programme there is no attempt to probe the privileged background of the teenagers who are in a position to spend a year on a Pacific island. Instead the interviewer's questions merely allow the teenagers to express their diluted version of a common fantasy. The toughest questions of the week are reserved for Richard Daley who, as an experienced politician on a goodwill tour, has no difficulty in dealing with them, particularly since even here Wogan gives only the appearance of an investigative interviewer and does not seriously disturb the atmosphere of friendly conversation.

However, these 'friends' generally have a purpose in contributing to the conversation. Guests do not appear on talk shows by chance. This is most obviously the case with Richard Daley, who quite openly admits that he is on a public relations tour for his home city, and Stefan Dennis on the Wednesday programme, who is introduced as being in the middle of a British publicity tour. But the other guests also had their reasons. Eartha Kitt had just published an autobiography, as had Linford Christie (who was also in the news for having captained the British athletics team at the World Cup in Barcelona the previous weekend, in which Britain had come third) and Bruce Forsyth had just published a book of golf stories.[7] He was also starting a new television show in a few months' time and was careful to mention this. Again the teenagers may seem to be an exception, along with the redoubtable Blatchford-Snell, but theirs was part of a continuing story. It also fitted very strongly with another aspect of such shows – their barely suppressed voyeurism.

The voyeuristic agenda

Implicit in all the conversations is the involvement of the audience as voyeurs, peering into the more private parts of public lives. Wogan himself is explicit about this, although slightly apologetic at the same time, when talking to the two teenagers. It emerges most clearly, though, in the remarkable conversation with Eartha Kitt. At this point the constraining structure of the programme nearly breaks down, as the singer talks of the sexual and emotional abuse she suffered as a child and how it affected her in later life. Almost breaking into tears, she only just manages to control her emotion and for an instant the conventional platitudes of Wogan's questions are threatened by a horrific reality – a reality that directly contradicts the cosy domestic atmosphere of the studio setting. Wogan, however, had already set the tone in his introduction (addressed directly to the audience) which is worth quoting in full since the way in which it manages to frame the interview – as a light-hearted conversation touching on serious topics – can be seen as a condensed version of the programme's general approach.

> How would you like to be rejected, ejected, dejected, used, accused, abused? You would? Then apply immediately for the job of Captain of the England cricket team. Seriously, seriously, chaps. One of my guests tonight has described her life in those six words. No, not 'Captain of the England cricket team' – rejected, ejected, dejected, and such. Even more, Orson Welles called her the most exciting woman in the world. Now, can you imagine having to live up to that? Walking around all day with your nostrils flaring, making little animal noises in the back of your throat. Come to think of it, she does! That's Eartha Kitt.

Thus the singer's horrific upbringing and the disappointments of her life are first of all compared to the problems of the captain of the unsuccessful national cricket team, and are then overtaken by comments about her sex appeal. The end of the interview is also interesting for its admission of the voyeuristic basis of the show, as well as for its modulation of tone, taking the show back into its light-hearted frame.

> Well, we're very glad that you've revealed so much of yourself and been unafraid to do so. And it's been a great pleasure to talk to you and thank you.

At one other point, again with a reference to sex, the show's premise is momentarily shaken. In a discussion of dangerous snakes, Stefan Dennis comments that the most dangerous one in Australia is 'the one-eyed trouser snake'. The joke – clearly beyond the bounds of the programme's respectability – causes a brief hiatus, with the audience unsure how to react and Wogan looking directly to the camera eliciting our collusion in his facial expression of 'what a childish thing to say'. The ideological significance of this voyeuristic appeal lies in the way in which it is harnessed by the ideological framework in an attempt to enact hegemonic appropriation. In other words, the viewer is enticed with the promise of voyeuristic pleasure, and thereby brought within the programme's consensual agenda. Voyeurism is the carrot, used to lead the viewer into the ideological mainstream.

Coming to you live

This look to camera (clearly expected by the programme producers, who know the ways in which Wogan deals with any 'problem' guests) raises the important question of how the audience is addressed. *Wogan* is broadcast live with a large studio audience (features which are common to most chat shows), but this audience is seldom seen. Wogan himself, in his introductions and during conversations, looks out and addresses comments either directly to the studio audience or to the domestic audience watching the television set. In doing this, and in acting the role of 'one of us' as opposed to the celebrities he will talk to, he attempts (or rather, the programme-makers attempt) to position us in a particular way. We are asked to share the jokes, the curiosity and, by implication, the attitudes which Wogan mediates. He represents us in the conversations. This will be clear in some of the comments noted above. It can also be illustrated by the talk with Mayor Daley.

The conversation with Daley is introduced as a conversation with a guest from a part of the United States which most Britons know only through film and television (and even that 'knowledge' tends to be restricted to myths about Prohibition gangsters). Daley is on the show, not because of anything he himself has done (in the way that most guests are chosen) but because he represents Chicago and is on a tour of Britain attempting to change attitudes towards his city. Wogan here takes on a double role. To Daley he provides a channel for letting him speak to the British television audience. For the audience, he gives expression of their myths and prejudices. Both aspects are made obvious in Wogan's first remarks.

> Now Richard, I'm not foolish. I know the reason you're here is to clean up Chicago's image. I mean, we do think, in our naïveté, there's still fellas around with moustaches, funny hats and tommy guns.

The talk soon moves on to a general discussion of crime in cities and how it should be dealt with. Wogan becomes the means of expression of mainstream, middle-class attitudes, defining the centre of society by marking out the deviants and becoming the spokesperson for those who totally reject such outsiders. This allows Daley's defence of the death penalty and life prison sentences for some drug-related crimes to pass unchallenged on moral grounds. The view that, for example, such an attitude represents an abdication of responsibility by an influential politician, does not get aired. Daley is allowed to define the discussion in his own terms. This, of course, is because his view is so consonant with the dominant attitudes within which the show functions. As with the Eartha Kitt interview, the ending is particularly revealing, as Wogan skilfully moves from crime to a light-hearted finish in one sentence.

> And finally can I ask you, so that we finish on an up-note, as it were, that if one isn't a drug smuggler or a criminal of any kind, why should one go on holiday to Chicago when you can go to Florida or the West Coast?

Here the audience's stereotypes, the identification with the social mainstream, and the exercising of structural closure are all worked into the one sentence.

A little more can usefully be said about the mode of address in this programme by commenting on the role of the studio audience. We have already noted the importance of such shows being live, and the presence of the audience is an important signifier of this. Terry Wogan's introductory comments frequently refer to topical events to which the audience reacts. The audience, however, has a more general and pervasive role. Wogan is, throughout these interviews, engaged in a conversation with three other participants. One is, of course, the studio guest. Another is the studio audience, to whom Wogan frequently appeals, sometimes to make a joke, sometimes to look for comic sympathy, sometimes to share their reaction, sometimes to attempt jokingly to quell their enthusiasm. The third participant is the television audience watching the programme in their homes. The significance of the studio audience is that it stands in for the home audience. Thus we, as domestic viewers, are not only given an indication of how to react, but Wogan's dialogue with the people in the studio can stand in for a dialogue with us. In addition, Wogan sometimes addresses the home audience directly by talking to the camera. Rather than being interpellated as passive observers of a continuing drama (as happens with much television fiction), this is a much stronger form of interpellation, constructing us as Terry's ideal audience. It works through the direct address to us in our homes, and through the only slightly less direct form of the address to the studio audience. Everything else which happens in the programme is set firmly within that framework. It is interesting to note that this form of four-cornered conversation (host, guest, studio audience and home audience) had already been a feature of Wogan's television style in his earlier panel game with celebrity guests, *Blankety Blank*.

A brief note will suffice on the rather restricted televisual style of the programme. Wogan walks on to a large studio stage, reacts to the studio audience and then talks to them and the camera. The rest of the programme takes place in the classic chat show setting of a smaller space with casual seating, placing host and guests in a semicircle in front of the audience and cameras. The camera style is barely noticeable, being the standard format of shots of the whole group contrasting with closer shots of individual speakers. Wogan's comments to camera are the only variations on this. The only other point worth noting is that often (usually at the beginning and ending of the programme) the studio set-up will be made obvious, with cameras and cables appearing in view, and a glimpse of the programme's resident band at one side playing the title music. Although at one time this would have been unusual in prime-time programming, nowadays it is much more common and can be seen as contributing to the programme's live feel, and thus to the professionalism of the host (which is itself a topic for his own jokes). Generally, then, the visual style of the programme works to create a strong framework, just as the content does.

Conclusion

The foregoing analysis of *Wogan* will have indicated the ideological forces at work in the programme, in particular the construction and reflection of a socially central, mainstream point of view. The style, content, structure and mode of address all contribute in important ways to the maintenance of this format. However, two important additional points must be made. The first is that this argument depends on showing a link between the programme's origin and the views which we have found expressed in it. In this case the link has already been referred to earlier in the chapter. The BBC's attempt to capture the early evening audience with an uncontroversial programme is enough to establish the reason for the ideological structure. This is a programme which works to reflect (and thus to reinforce) the dominating centre of society. There is a sense in which the unvarying topic of *Wogan* is not the guests but the audience, as the programme marks out the social consensus. This process is not a simple one, however. It appears indirectly through Wogan's questions, jokes and comments. It also appears in the choice of guest – sometimes as a straightforward celebration of achievement but also sometimes by selecting a guest who, as an outsider, defines the limits of the consensus. The BBC cannot be seen as an always unproblematic conveyor of dominant views, despite its position in British society. There is always room for the exception. In this case, however, problematic content is studiously avoided.

A contrast can be identified here with the American talk shows of Oprah Winfrey and Phil Donohue. Both place their emphasis on the voyeuristic aspect of conversation and tend to bring out into the open far more controversial topics than those which Wogan addresses. This is partly because they are not situated so near the centre of the broadcasting establishment, but it is also indicative of a rather different ideological strategy in a different ideological situation, centred on the varying roles of the concept of freedom in Britain and America, and on the role of populism in American society. Freedom has a central place in American ideology, to the extent that the word can even be used to justify what are plainly illiberal practices – as in the support given to non-communist dictatorships in Asia and Latin America, or, in a more specific domestic context, the support given to the freedom to own weapons. This carries over into other areas, such as religious and personal freedom, which can easily make appeals to this ideological core. In the talk shows referred to above, it manifests itself as the standard of action. The shows are, in effect, presenting America to itself, and thus their display of individual variety becomes easily mobilized as a display of essential American values, even when the views expressed by guests are clearly minority and unpopular views. Similarly, populism is expressed by the presenter's reliance on the audience for support and active participation (which are a much more important part of the show than they are in *Wogan*).

The second point to be made in concluding is that, as always, reception depends on the audience. We have been outlining the dominant structures in the programme, but these are not impossible to avoid. The conversation with Eartha Kitt, for example, allows for (and even to some extent encourages) a feminist reaction, just as the social privilege expressed by Martin Popplewell in the Wednesday programme allows for a reaction rather different to the one he clearly expects. *Wogan* typifies much television output in the way it allows a certain (although fairly limited) variety of voices to be heard (Mimi White refers to this as television's 'regulated ideological plurality')[8] and thus allows space for a certain amount of variety of reaction, despite its powerful framework of consensus. More generally, a simple reaction of displeasure can result from rejection of the programme's ideological force. In *Wogan*, pleasure has ideological implications.

8 Decentred biography

During the greater part of the twentieth century the most influential media format has been that of the narrative film. This is not just because for much of this century it has been a major source of entertainment for millions of people in countries round the world, but also because it has had a central role in developing the styles and content of popular, visual fiction. Its influence is evident on television drama of all kinds, on advertising, on music video, on fashion, and even (although not so obviously) on written fiction. Its ideological role is particularly interesting. Film is a massively expensive medium. It therefore has to appeal to a large enough audience to recoup these costs. However, film is also regarded by many as potentially a very personal medium in which film-makers may be able to express themselves. The non-specific term 'film-makers' has been chosen deliberately since the creative input into any film can come from a disparate group of people. Producer, director, scriptwriter, cinematographer, actor, composer, and art director can all work together (or in conflict) to produce the final product. This makes the ideological forces at work on a film potentially very complex, particularly since international co-productions are becoming increasingly common, especially in Europe.

There have been a number of ideological analyses of films published, usually restricted to the more popular end of the market.[1] An interesting recent example of this is the chapter on the films of Steven Spielberg in the second edition (1988) of Robert Kolker's *A Cinema of Loneliness*.[2] The title and subtitle of this chapter will indicate the direction of his analysis – 'In the Patriarch's Bosom: Steven Spielberg and the Politics of Recuperation'. Kolker sees Spielberg's films (including *Jaws*, *Close Encounters of the Third Kind*, *E.T.* and *Raiders of the Lost Ark*) as central examples of American popular culture.

> Spielberg's films constitute a factory of ideological production, the great imaginary of the eighties, full of images the culture wanted to see, images and narratives that expressed the culture. The frequency, success, and influence of his films during a relatively short period of time have made them a kind of encyclopedia of desire, a locus of representations to which audiences wished to be called.[3]

Such an approach is concerned with content at a fairly obvious level, and with narrative structure. It is also, as will be clear from the quotation, based on a rather simplistic equation of popular film content with audience desire, assuming a straightforward correspondence model of ideological reflection in which these massively popular films can be read as showing how audiences fantasized about themselves.

Rather than add to such studies of popular films, we will expand the analytical project by looking at a film which, although produced by one of the major Hollywood film companies (United Artists), was a critical rather than a popular success. It is a more complex film than those of, for example, Steven Spielberg, but also a more violent one, and as such should be a particularly interesting subject for ideological analysis. The film is *Raging Bull*, directed by Martin Scorsese.[4]

Raging Bull

Acclaimed by film critics when first released in November 1980, *Raging Bull* has, if anything, increased its reputation over the years. At the end of 1989 it was voted best film of the decade in several critics' polls, both in the United States and in Britain. It has an interesting production background. Scorsese had established himself as a leading American film director during the seventies with such films as *Mean Streets* (1973), *Alice Doesn't Live Here Anymore* (1974) and *Taxi Driver* (1976). By the end of the seventies, however, after the commercial failure of the hugely expensive *New York, New York* (1977), he was finding it difficult to get his projects financed and began shooting *Raging Bull* thinking that it might be his last film. As he said in an interview,

> I put everything I knew and everything I felt into that film. I thought it was the end of my career. I figured that was it. I thought 'to hell with it'.[5]

The film shows the real-life story of the New York-Italian boxer Jake La Motta, but it is no ordinary Hollywood biopic. Not only was it based on La Motta's ghost-written autobiography, but the boxer himself was involved in the production, being credited in the film as 'creative consultant'.

Although Scorsese is often seen as the archetypal New Hollywood film author, expressing his own concerns on film, his collaborators on *Raging Bull* are of crucial importance. Foremost is the star of the film, Robert De Niro. He had already worked with Scorsese in three films and was rewarded with the Academy Award for Best Actor for his performance in this film. Coming from a similar New York-Italian background as Scorsese (and, of course, as La Motta), De Niro had shown himself to be the ideal working partner for Scorsese's New York-based films. The script is credited to Paul Schrader and Mardik Martin, both of whom had previously written for Scorsese, although De Niro and the director both contributed extensively to it as well. Also worth mentioning are cinematographer Michael Chapman and film editor Thelma Schoonmaker, both of whose contributions to the film are very obvious and very important. The cost of the film was about $14 million. More detail on its background can be found in Marion Weiss's book *Martin Scorsese*,[6] and interviews with Scorsese himself concerning the film can be found in Mary Pat Kelly's *Martin Scorsese: the First Decade*.[7]

Raging Bull traces the history of the New York boxer Jake La Motta (played by Robert De Niro) who, because of his indestructibility, became known as 'the Bronx Bull'. His manager is his younger brother Joey (played by Joe Pesci). Jake's aim is to become the World Middleweight Champion and he wants to achieve this by his own skill, not with the help of the gangsters who control the championship and who try to persuade him to cooperate. Despite winning his fights, he is not allowed a shot at the title and eventually has to agree to work with the gangsters, throwing a fight in 1947 and thereby getting his chance at the World Championship which he wins in 1949. After this, however, he goes into decline, losing the title in 1951 to his great rival Sugar Ray Robinson.

Alongside this professional career, we are shown Jake's private life. As the film begins in 1941 he is married, but falls in love with a local blonde teenager, Vicki (played by Cathy Moriarty), whom he is not able to marry until 1945. He develops an irrational jealousy of Vicki which reaches a peak in 1950 causing him to break with his brother, just as his career is going into decline. In the mid-fifties Jake opens a nightclub in Miami but, soon after Vicki finally leaves him, he receives a short prison sentence for introducing men to underage girls. After his release he makes a living as a stand-up comic in small bars, and a chance meeting in 1958 leads to reconciliation with Joey. The film ends with Jake rehearsing his nightclub act in a dressing-room in 1964. The first part of this final scene also began the film, acting as an introduction to the whole story.

A structure of absences

Such a synopsis of the plot may not convey its episodic structure. The transition between one scene and another is not the logical progression of the traditional Hollywood film in which questions set up in one scene (how is the hero going to react? what will be the effect of the action just seen?) are answered in the next, or the next but one. Richard Combs has written of this film that it seems to have been made out of an impatience with all the usual trappings of cinema, with plot, psychology, and an explanatory approach to character.[8]

We jump from one scene to another with little obvious connection other than the chronology of Jake's life. No background is given and we have to fill in the detail of his life from various brief and sometimes enigmatic comments. And this is despite the use of a technique more commonly seen in documentary films – the explanatory titles telling us where and when scenes take place. The film opens in Jake's dressing-room in the Brabazon Plaza Hotel, with the titles 'New York 1964'. We see him going over his nightclub act, ending with the words 'That's entertainment' as the titles say 'Jake La Motta 1964'. We then hear him repeating 'That's entertainment' as the scene changes and we see a much younger Jake in a boxing match receiving several savage punches on his face. The titles say 'Jake La Motta 1941', and from a radio commentary on the soundtrack we hear that he is fighting Jimmy Reeves. After Reeves gets a points victory, despite being knocked out by Jake in the closing seconds of the match, we suddenly jump to a city street and the titles 'The Bronx, New York City, 1941'. At no point do we get any biographical background about either his personal life or his professional career. As the film progresses this jumping from one scene to another becomes more marked. The seemingly informative titles allow us to place scenes in chronological order, but much information which biographical narratives usually include (Jake's interior life, in particular his motivation, and the detailed background to the events we see) is withheld. We end up with a film about a famous character which tells us remarkably little about that person's mental life (a topic which is conventionally part of any biography, although by definition it is the one part of a life which is inaccessible to the biographer). When Jake's obsessive jealousy disrupts his personal life, very little preparation is given. There are hints of his sexual inadequacies and of his (perhaps consequential) obsession with winning the championship, but this is not enough to prepare viewers for the ferocity of the scene in which he not only violently attacks Joey in front of his children, but also knocks out Vicki with a punch to her face.

This gives us a very open film, that is, one in which judgments about the principal characters and actions are not suggested for us, in the manner of more conventional films. (A useful comparison, given the similarity of subject matter, can be made with the Sylvester Stallone boxing films – *Rocky*, 1976, and its various sequels, and *Paradise Alley*, 1978 – all of which are made in a very traditional manner). We have to make our own guesses about Jake's motives, and these will depend on our own ideological placings much more than is usual in mainstream American films. The overall episodic structure adds to this. Despite a technique which films frequently use to effect a strong narrative closure – beginning the film with a scene from the end of the chronological development – this narrative is left relatively open. The chronological beginning and ending are fairly arbitrary. We could, for example, have begun with Jake's first professional fight, or with his childhood. Both would have given a more 'logical' place to start, that is, one which would be closer to the conventions of narrative. Similarly we could have ended at a later point in his life. La Motta went on to have a minor career in film and television. Even before 1964 he had appeared in a very small role in a famous Hollywood film – *The Hustler* (1960) – and he is probably best known to audiences nowadays for his role as the neighbour in the television comedy series *ALF*. Instead of showing the successes in this show-business career, or only showing his boxing career, the film stops as he is in the process of developing the second career (and gives no indication of his Hollywood life).

Violence, masculinity and women

Although the structure is comparatively open, the content of the film is less so. Certain fairly obvious preoccupations recur in the film – the heavily subordinate role of women in a strongly macho society and their two-dimensional portrayal, the related fear of homosexuality (made clear in many jokes throughout the film), the restricted vocabulary (resulting in constant swearing), the absence of legitimate authority (there is very little evidence of the legal authorities, the main figure of power being the mafia boss Tommy Como). Along with this we are shown a very negative representation of the family – we never see Jake's parents, the family settings we do see become arenas of violence, and by the end, despite the apparent reconciliation with Joey, the overwhelming impression of Jake is of a man alone, without family or friends. In addition to these elements there is the portrayal of violence as a constant but unpredictable fact of life, being the only satisfactory means of expression for the principal characters, and expressing not just their own physical power, but more broadly, their *lack* of power in a society in which they have become marginalized – socially, economically and politically. These thematic preoccupations will be recognized by those who are familiar with Scorsese's other films, in particular those set in New York (even the comedy *After Hours* is based around the same themes, although in comic inversion, as in the procession of women who threaten the hero with physical violence).

The point, however, about these themes is that they are made very obvious in *Raging Bull*. This is clearest in the treatment of women. At various points in the film, the double standards of Jake and Joey are foregrounded. They are shown to be highly possessive husbands who dislike their wives even mentioning the fact that a particular boxer is handsome (Jake is driven to destroy the face of boxer Tony Janiro after Vicki has referred to him as good-looking). At the same time they are shown to apply very different standards of sexual morality to themselves (Jake's romance with Vicki begins when he is still married to his first wife). Although there is not an overt narrational condemnation of this, which leaves the audience the possibility of a wide range of reaction, the irrationality of the male characters' behaviour is fully displayed. In other words, rather than taking up an explicit moral position towards these actions, the film simply displays them. In doing this it is a good example of what Althusser regarded as the ideological role of art, as he described it in his 'Letter on Art'.

> What art makes us *see*, and therefore gives to us in the form of '*seeing*', '*perceiving*' and '*feeling*' (which is not the form of '*knowing*'), is the *ideology* from which it is born, in which it bathes, from which it detaches itself as art, and to which it *alludes*.[9]

Althusser's comments do not work well for all forms and genres of art, but for the kind of seemingly detached and 'realistic' approach which we can see in *Raging Bull* it is a useful comment. Rather than being buried within ideology (as, for example, the *Rocky* films are, with their unquestioning portrayal of masculinity and achievement), or pointing up their ideological structure in any obvious way (we will find an example of this approach in the following chapter), Scorsese's film shows up the ideological situation of Jake La Motta and makes it unfamiliar by letting us see it in a privileged fashion. Althusser's notion of 'allusion' then becomes particularly apt.

But of course the ideological origins of this film lie not in the America of the 1940s but in the America of the late 1970s. If we list some of the determining factors on the making of the film, then its complex relationship to the dominant ideology of the United States in the late seventies should become clear. First we must consider Scorsese's origins. As a New York-Italian, that is, as a member of a sub-cultural group with a strong identity, Scorsese's own ideological position is likely to be at one remove from the American mainstream. The fact that La Motta and De Niro share this background suggests that it has had some impact on the film. A second factor lies in notions of artistic professionalism. We have already seen (in the previous chapter) that professional ideologies can play an important role in the shaping of cultural products. Here we can suggest that the related notions of film as a medium for artistic self-expression and as (in some sense) a witness of reality have pushed the film-makers towards a particular type of product. In other words, the professional ideology of the film-makers has led to a particular kind of justification, one which emphasizes their own integrity over considerations of commercial appeal.

A third determining factor is the historical context. The late seventies was a period in which the United States was still recovering from the ideological crisis brought on by the oil shortage, the Vietnam War, and the Watergate scandal. The film appeared as the Reagan era was about to begin. The uncertainties of the seventies are expressed here in several ways – the foregrounding of violence, the destruction of the family, the self-conscious examination of masculinity, the absence of political or social solutions, and the undermining of authority. When we add to this that the formative period of many of the collaborators on this film (such as Scorsese, De Niro and Schrader) was the sixties, with its radical optimism, then the relation between *Raging Bull* and its context should be clarified. It appears as a film about the forties and fifties, in which sixties' radicalism is mediated by seventies' disillusion.

It is important to note that Scorsese's previous successes (particularly with De Niro in *Taxi Driver*) were important in allowing him and his collaborators a certain amount of ideological space in which to work. His reputation (and De Niro's) allowed a more complex and subversive film to be made than would have been acceptable to a film company if he had been an unknown and untested director.

The significations of style

Already, then, we can see how the film links strong thematic concerns with an open structure, and how this is related to its ideological determinations. When we add to this a consideration of style, it becomes all the more complex. To describe fully the style of any film would take more space that is available here, but a number of prominent features of *Raging Bull* can be listed.

1. It is made in black and white.
2. As noted earlier, documentary-style titles are used to give locations and dates.
3. A fairly mobile camera style is used, particularly in the fight scenes.
4. Brief slow-motion sequences occur regularly.
5. Still images, in the style of sports journalism, are used in many of the fight scenes.

6. A complex soundtrack uses, in addition to many pieces of popular music of the forties, orchestral extracts from popular Italian operas by the nineteenth-century composer Pietro Mascagni.

A rather different aspect of the film's style is its references to other films, that is, its *intertextuality*. In the opening and closing scenes in his Brabazon Plaza dressing-room, Jake rehearses a speech from the 1954 film *On the Waterfront*. In this speech the hero, a former boxer called Terry Molloy (played in the film by Marlon Brando), complains to his brother and former manager Charlie (played by Rod Steiger) that he should have helped him more in his boxing career, instead of getting him to cooperate with the gangsters in fixing a fight. More generally the film echoes the structure of the classic boxing films of the forties, such as *Body and Soul* (1947) and *The Set-Up* (1949) – all of which were made in black and white. There is also an explicit reference to the 1939 film *Of Mice and Men*, a film based on John Steinbeck's story of a simple-minded but immensely strong man who keeps getting into trouble because of his temper. And, of course, the phrase heard at the beginning of the film – 'That's entertainment' – refers us to Hollywood in general, and the film musical in particular.

When these stylistic elements are put together, the result is a rather intriguing mixture. The use of black and white and the scene-setting titles recall classic documentary technique, enforcing the film's claims to realism (claims made all the stronger by its biographical basis). Similar to this is the use of still images, composed and lit like the sports photographs which regularly appear in newspapers. On the other hand, the references to other films, and again, the use of black and white, strengthen the links to fiction, setting the film in a history of dramatic boxing stories (most of which are centred around the hero's conflicts with fight-fixing gangsters). Slow-motion as an expressive technique, however, takes us into the area of the psychological film, making us concentrate on the hero's reactions. It is used to put us in the exact position of a central character (usually Jake, but on one occasion Joey) so that we see what they see but with the visuals emphasized so as to make it appear as though we are witnessing what is for the filmic character an important moment of heightened awareness. The use of 'classical' music adds another element, at once nostalgic and noble (although here there is even more room for varying interpretations), relating the film to 'serious' accounts of heroism and tragedy. This is most apparent in the almost operatic intensity of the scene of Jake's fight with Marcel Cerdan when he finally wins his world title.

The style of the film, then, introduces conflicting discourses — documentary truth, cinematic history, and artistic seriousness — which stir up the thematic concerns already noted. In addition to this the dwelling on violence links *Raging Bull* to the many popular films of the seventies which pushed the experience of cinematic violence to a new extreme. The appeal of these different discourses is complex, at once pandering to the knowledgeable viewer's self-esteem, bringing into question the whole apparatus of filmic biography and media representation, and playing to the desire to see physical violence. The danger is that these stylistic techniques lead merely to an aestheticization of the content and allow the viewer (as well as the film-makers) to retain a safe ethical and emotional distance from the film.

A fragmentary address

This leads us on to the question of how the film addresses its viewers. Rather than a single form, the stylistic mix gives a multiple address. At one point we are being addressed as if we were the viewers of a compilation documentary, at the next as if we were watching a classic Hollywood film with all the knowledge (and desires) which that implies. At other moments we are asked to share the precise point of view, and to some extent the mental reaction, of the main characters. There is even a short sequence in the style of a home movie (this is the only colour sequence in the film) showing Jake's personal life in the mid-forties, just as his career is flourishing. In other words, the film works against allowing us to settle into one coherent viewing position. In ideological terms, the interpellation is contradictory. Not only that, but at the end of the day, the film is non-informative. Despite the apparatus of documentary with its implied knowledge of the subject-matter, despite the links to classic films with their unproblematical stereotyped characters, despite the cinematic techniques of psychological realism with their claim to privileged access to the hero's mind, this film denies us knowledge of the hero's motivations. The centre of the biography — Jake's personality — becomes a cypher. We can make guesses as to its solution, but they remain only guesses. Thus the film becomes ideologically unsettling. It produces various subject positions for the audience and also describes a central character who seems to lack the necessary basis for a coherent identity and yet whose seemingly unmotivated actions form the plot.

This links up with another aspect of the film. In the viewing or reading of any work of fiction there is a process of identification at work. We look for a way into the text by identifying with characters. In the conventional popular film this is made easy for us. The hero or heroine is presented unambiguously and we happily follow their progress through the plot. Ideologically, such a process will tend to make us share the values and judgments which that central character represents, even if we only do this half-heartedly for the duration of the film. In *Raging Bull*, however, there is a problem. Jake's actions are frequently so extreme (most notably in his jealous rage against Joey and his violence against Vicki) and are given so little motivation, that a comfortable identification with him is extremely difficult – and this is despite the use of the slow-motion point-of-view shots mentioned above, which would normally have tended to strengthen our identification with him. It is not surprising that some viewers find this not only a very unsettling and uncomfortable film to watch, but one which leaves them puzzled at the end, not knowing what to think.

Content

Raging Bull, then, is a film which displays its ideological formations and refuses to provide answers to the problems it reveals (particularly concerning violence and gender). It becomes a biography without a centre, as the knowledge necessary fully to understand the 'hero' is withheld. Viewers are placed in an uncomfortable position, being left to complete the narrative and to make sense of its stylistic features. The oblique relationship to dominant ideological trends explains why this film did not capture a large ready-made audience. This may make it sound as if it is a classic subversive text. The problem there, however, is that it avoids any solutions. This can simply leave an audience puzzled, and no doubt contributed to the film's box office failure. Also, its claims to artistic integrity (bolstered by the biblical quote which Scorsese adds at the end) can function as a way of defusing any subversive content. The film becomes reduced to a personal statement by a creative artist. The eclectic style becomes a signifier of individuality, just as the biographical details are read by some as Scorsese's autobiographical statement, with his escape into film-making seen as equivalent to Jake's escape into boxing. In both cases success allows them to transcend their New York-Italian origins. As in many biographical approaches to the creative arts, this ideology of the artist is, in effect, a way of making safe the subversions of the work of art itself. The artist can become the excuse for the art, and the safe investigation of the artist can replace the uncomfortable confrontation with the work itself, and with the society out of which it has emerged.

What the foregoing analysis should establish is that, in complex cultural products such as *Raging Bull*, ideology works in ways which are not always easy to apprehend and which may be contradictory. Such works do not reflect ideology in any straightforward manner and their lack of popular appeal can be related directly to this. Their complex structures, however, do allow audiences to interact with them in a variety of ways which can provide compensatory pleasures beyond those of ideological recognition and confirmation.

9 Fictional history

Of all the cultural forms examined in this book, the novel is the one with the longest and most respectable pedigree. It is also the one which conventionally is valued most highly, and so the use of ideological analysis to study it is likely to arouse opposition. However, this opposition must be seen as ideological in itself. If the account outlined in the opening chapters is sound, then all kinds of writing, whether formal or informal, literary or non-literary, fictional or factual, will – to some extent at least – show the influence of ideology. The question is not whether literature is ideological but to what exent it is ideological.

Some writers have suggested that by its very nature the novel is profoundly ideological. Lennard J. Davis, in his book *Resisting Novels*, states that 'novels do not depict life, they depict life as it is represented by ideology'.[1] He goes on to argue that the novel's depiction of space, character, and dialogue, as well as the mechanisms of plot, are all simplifications in the name of ideology, deeply implicated in a particular view of life. Thus of character he writes:

> the simplification of personality required to produce a character in a novel is itself once again an ideological statement about the role of the individual in relation to society since the early modern period.[2]

Similarly, when discussing plot he argues that,

> plot in narratives, and most particularly novels, helps readers to believe that there is an order in the world.[3]

This approach is extremely broad, dismissing novels out of hand as little more than a form of propaganda. It makes it difficult to say anything useful about the manifold differences between novels (most of Davis's examples are from traditional works). A more important criticism, however, is that it is based on an empiricist approach to reality. In order to demonstrate the novel's simplifications, Davis has to assume that his own knowledge of reality is non-ideological and 'scientific'.

Terry Eagleton has suggested a more flexible approach, beginning with the premise that literature has a distinctive relationship to ideology.

> Literature, one might argue, is the most revealing mode of experiential access to ideology that we possess. It is in literature, above all, that we observe in a peculiarly complex, coherent, intensive and immediate fashion the workings of ideology in the textures of lived experience of class-societies.[4]

Precisely how this works is not so clear but later in the same essay he attempts to describe it in this way.

> Literature is a peculiar mode of linguistic organization which, by a particular 'disturbance' of conventional modes of signification, so foregrounds certain modes of sense-making as to allow us to perceive the ideology in which they inhere.[5]

In other words, by making our awareness of the world in some way different (sometimes the word *defamiliarization* is used to express this process) literature can make obvious the ideological structures of our world. Or rather, as Eagleton says, it *allows* such a form of perception. The novel, then, can be seen as a form which allows some kind of privileged insight into the ideological structures in which it is embedded. However, by its very reputation, literature tends to play against such readings. The concept of the romantic artist expressing her or, more usually, his deepest soul and using an unfettered imagination is deeply ingrained in our culture. It works against any attempt at social interpretation, insisting on the artist's autonomy. But even when such an account of romantic creativity is rejected as naïve and simplistic, the varieties of artistic creation will force us to take *some* account of the individual when considering the cultural forms of literature. This can make the ideological analysis of such texts problematical. The various vectors of ideology, individuality, originality and intertextuality (that is, the text's relation to other texts) can intertwine in complex ways.

In order to see how such theories might be used, we will look at a recent novel rather than the traditional or early twentieth-century examples with which many theorists (such as Eagleton, Jameson and Davis) concern themselves. Since the 1960s the novel has become a highly self-conscious form of narrative, and studying an example of this kind may be more revealing than simply performing one more analysis of traditional novel-writing.

A Maggot

Our example is a novel written by a well-known English writer, but which has a particularly complex relationship to other texts and other kinds of writing: *A Maggot* by John Fowles. Born in 1926 near Southend in Essex, Fowles studied languages at Oxford University and then became a teacher. He established his literary reputation during the sixties with three novels – *The Collector* (1963), *The Magus* (1966) and *The French Lieutenant's Woman* (1969). All three were very successful and were made into films (although only the third became at all well-known in this form). His later books have included *The Ebony Tower* (1974), *Daniel Martin* (1977), and *Mantissa* (1982). *A Maggot* was published in Britain in September 1985, with a paperback edition appearing in 1986.

The action of *A Maggot* takes place, for the most part, in England in 1736. The story concerns the disappearance of the son of an unnamed English Duke. This son, who had a passionate interest in occult philosophy, was last known to have been travelling from London to Devon under the name of 'Mr Bartholomew'. Accompanying him were four companions – his mute servant and childhood friend Dick, a prostitute known as Fanny but whose name is later revealed to be Rebecca Hocknell, a fifty-one-year-old actor Francis Lacy who on the journey pretended to be Bartholomew's uncle, and David Jones, a thirty-six-year-old Welshman who on the journey pretended to be a former marine, Sergeant Farthing. Bartholomew was last seen at the beginning of May, 1736, near Exmoor where Dick is found hanged, presumed to be an act of suicide. Lacy is found to have been paid to act the part of the uncle so as to disguise Bartholomew's real identity. Rebecca is traced to Manchester where she is found to be the wife of a Quaker, John Lee, and to be living according to that religion. The story ends with the birth of her daughter Ann, on 29 February 1737. At the centre of this story is a mysterious event in a cave on Exmoor – the last occasion on which Bartholomew was seen. This event and the circumstances surrounding it remain a mystery at the end of the novel. The only descriptions are given through the eyes, understanding and vocabulary of the eighteenth-century characters involved. Whether this is a supernatural event involving time travel (as Bartholomew hints) or simply an event too far from the normal experience of an eighteenth-century character to be easily explained, or even a straightforward happening which is witnessed under the influence of hallucinatory drugs, is not made clear.

The telling of the tale

Crucial to any description of this novel is an account of how the story is told, that is, its narration. The traditional novel consists of a third-person narration. Actions and events are described from the point of view of an unseen observer who can see any action, and who has knowledge of the thoughts and emotions of the characters involved. This forms the frame which can include other points of view, most usually that which is represented by characters' dialogue, but sometimes also written comments, as in letters, for example. Colin MacCabe has referred to this format as that of 'the classic realist text'.[6] It is realist since the omniscient third person framing narration is taken as giving the 'truth' of the situation which the novel describes, even if that 'true situation' is fictional. The embedded elements of dialogue are judged according to how they fit with the framing account. If dialogue contradicts that account, then the character speaking is judged to be lying. For MacCabe, such a structure has ideological implications since it cannot account for contradictions, assuming reality (even fictional reality) to be perfectly understandable and non-contradictory.

A *Maggot* departs from the structure of the classic realist text. The story is revealed through various voices, some of which we are encouraged to believe, but some of which contradict each other without any final judgment being given on them. Almost two-thirds of the novel is in the form of interviews, with Ayscough, a lawyer working for the unnamed aristocrat, questioning various witnesses, trying to find out what happened. These interviews are given in the question (Q) and answer (A) form in which Ayscough's clerk notes them, which is then sent to his employer. An example is the following, taken from the interrogation of Lacy.

> Q. Before all else you shall answer me this. Knew you Mr.
>   Bartholomew was under false name?
> A. I did.
> Q. Knew you who he truly was?
> A. I did not, and do not, to this day.
> Q. On what occasion did you last see him?
> A. The first of May last.[7]

It will be clear from this that Fowles is careful to adopt an eighteenth-century style for these accounts, giving them the appearance of historical documents.

In addition to this, almost a quarter of the book is written in a third-person narration. However, this does not give the novel the firm non-contradictory framework which might be expected. This is partly because this narration takes two forms, neither of which is the omniscient style of the traditional novel. The commonest form is the fairly distant, descriptive style of an observer who can see but does not have access to characters' thoughts, and who is not present at certain key events, most notably the mysterious central event. This style is most obvious in the opening section. The following extract comes from the first description of the central characters' journeying into Devon.

> The newcomer reins in some ten yards short of the leading younger gentleman, then touches his hat and turns his horse to walk beside him. He says something, and the gentleman nods, without looking at him. The newcomer touches his hat again, then pulls aside and waits

until the last pair come abreast of him. They stop, and the newcomer leans across and unfastens the leading-line of the pack-horse from its ring behind the saddle. No friendly word seems spoken, even here. The newcomer then takes his place, now leading the pack-horse, at the rear of the procession; and very soon it is as if he has always been there, one more mute limb of the indifferent rest.[8]

But this is not the only form of narration. Mixed in with it is what seems to be the clear voice of the author. Sometimes this takes the form of explicit recognition of the historical context of the novel – a novel about the early eighteenth century, written in the late twentieth century. The beginning of a paragraph in this opening section will make this clear.

A twentieth-century mind, could it have journeyed back and taken on the sensibilities and eyes of those two better-class travellers riding that day into the town, must have felt. . .[9]

This form is most obvious in the 'Prologue' and 'Epilogue' in which the author directly addresses us, his twentieth-century readers, telling us something about the writing of the novel and of the author's opinions.

Dissent is a universal human phenomenon, yet that of Northern Europe and America is, I suspect, our most precious legacy to the world.[10]

In addition to these narrational forms, there are letters written by various characters, mainly from Ayscough to his employer, but also those from other investigators to Ayscough. Some of these are from real historical characters, such as the famous eighteenth-century blind mathematician Nicholas Saunderson.

The reality of history

The question to concern us here is how this heterogeneity of voices is linked to ideology. By presenting a series of personal accounts, none of which is given omniscient status, the novel is emphasizing our dependence on personal experience. Just as history is dependent on our interpretation of documents from another age, rather than being something we 'directly' experience, so the novel's 'reality' (that is, the series of events which it describes) is only made available to us through the very partial views of other people. Thus the novel works to relativize knowledge.

This process is clearest when we consider the mysterious central event which Ayscough investigates. The first description is given in the account of the interview with David Jones.[11] He tells of how he met Rebecca immediately after the incident and, although he did not witness it himself, she told him about it. When we reach Rebecca's own account she says that she made up the story she told Jones, and proceeds to tell what she now says is the truth.[12] However, like any person describing something, she is limited by her vocabulary and by her previous experience. This is shown when she describes what seems to be a space ship of some kind. She says it was like a giant maggot and gives this description of it, after being prompted by a question from Ayscough.

> Q. I'll know more of this maggot. What appearance had it?
> A. Of white, yet not of flesh, as it were wood japanned, or fresh-tinned metal, large as three coaches end to end, or more, its head with the eye larger still; and I did see other eyes along its sides that shone also, tho' less, through a greenish glass. And at its end there was four great funnels black as pitch, so it might vent its belly forth there.[13]

She goes on to interpret the experience in terms of her religion and it becomes clear that for her the event has come to function as a turning point in her life, an experience of religious revelation. We, however, are left with only her eighteenth-century account of an event that would seem to be more at home in a twentieth-century science fiction story. (It has clear links with two famous science fiction films – *Things to Come* and *2001: A Space Odyssey* – as well as with the television series *Dr Who*). Not only this, but given the fact that the event has assumed such a major status in her own life, it is quite possible that her account – even on her own terms – has become highly distorted as she has 'read' the event in the light of her later development.

The relativity of accounts is very important, since ideology usually works in the opposite direction, making knowledge seem absolute. We noted in chapter 1 that ideology typically works to turn the historical into the natural. The traditional novel does this by giving its narration the status of realist description. *A Maggot*, on the other hand, does the opposite. It emphasizes how human knowledge, even basic description, is profoundly historical. This reflects back on the work of Fowles himself, emphasizing the status of his writing. Despite its pseudo-historical language (and very few readers will have the historical knowledge necessary to judge how accurate is his eighteenth-century pastiche – what matters is the *appearance* of accuracy), this is a modern creation, a product of Britain in the 1980s. From this point of view, the strange happening in the cave on Exmoor can be taken as a paradigm of cultural experience. The event has its own determinations, but these determinations are now impossible for us to discover, particularly since the meaning of the event varies according to the ideological situation of whoever is describing it. Even readers now, at the end of the twentieth century, will find it difficult to avoid settling on one particular interpretation, regardless of the fact that Fowles does not give us enough information to make such a decision. And whether we read it as a religious event, a hallucination, an example of science fiction or, indeed, whether we give it some other interpretation, will say more about our own situation than that of the author or his characters.

Contextualizing the author

As a novel written in Britain in the early 1980s, we should be able to find traces of the ideological forces at work at that time. This is not, however, a straightforward task. As already noted, the novel is a cultural form which mediates ideology in a particularly complex way. Fowles's own comments make clear his distance from the prevailing orthodoxies. In the epilogue he not only confesses to being an atheist but gives his opinion on the state of Western society.

> A historically evolved outward form, adapted as in a plant or animal to cope with one set of conditions, is doomed when a new set appears; as in my view not only the United, but Western society as a whole, only too plainly shows.[14]

(The reference to the United Society is to the religious sect, known more commonly as the Shakers, which was founded by Ann Lee, Rebecca's daughter born at the end of the novel – thus the fiction of the novel ends with the birth of a 'real' historical character.) Yet, despite these apocalyptic views, the ideological currents traceable in the novel are more concerned with life as it is now, in the late twentieth century. Three themes are particularly notable – the attitude to history, the treatment of women, and the role of the intellectual. All are bound up very closely with Fowles's own situation.

The attitude to history has already been commented upon in reference to the way the novel emphasizes the contingency of all historical knowledge. This thematic concern can be expanded. If we set the book firmly in its own historical context – Britain in the early and middle eighties – then such an attitude becomes more political. In the early years of the decade Britain was, of course, involved in a war in the South Atlantic. The overt calling on tradition which was common at that time, and which was used by the government in various ways (ranging from the call for a return to 'Victorian' family values to the attempt to deny the multicultural nature of contemporary British society), is at odds with the novel's account of history. In this sense *A Maggot* can be seen as oppositional – although only if this fairly sophisticated comparison between context and content is made. Some reviewers in 1985 certainly saw it in that way. Anthony Burgess wrote that it 'serves, as all literature should, the forces of subversion'.[15] Pat Rogers described it as 'Fowles's most political work of fiction to date'.[16] Working against this is the novel's setting in a distant historical period, which easily allows the reader to interpret social comment as of historical relevance only.

The treatment of women is best seen by the changing role of Rebecca. Her development in the novel becomes virtually a model for feminist awakening, changing from sexual servant of the males to the strongest and freest-thinking character in the novel. Although the mystery, the question to be answered, at the beginning of the story concerns the Duke's son, by the end his fate has become an irrelevance, replaced in the novel's structure by the transformation of Rebecca. In a very real sense she, not the Exmoor disappearance, is the subject of the novel. Even the strange event becomes important because of its effect on her, rather than as a mystery in itself. This alters our relationship with the lawyer, Ayscough. In the first part of the story, he stands in for us – he asks our questions and attempts to sort out the facts in this mystery with which we are faced. By the end, the gap between his point of view (which becomes increasingly 'historicized' as the novel progresses, and thus alienated from the late twentieth-century readership) and ours becomes almost insurmountable. Consider this comment from his final letter to his master. He is discussing Rebecca's character.

> She was never, as is the commonalty of her sex, brought to know God's wisdom in decreeing for them their natural place as helpmeet to man, in house and home alone.[17]

The view that women are ordained by religious authority to be domestic servants for men is in direct conflict not only with Rebecca's testimony but with the comments which the narrator occasionally interpolates.

If the novel is thus regarded as an investigation of the principal female character, rather than the detective mystery it at first appears to be, then it fits in well with Fowles's other novels. From *The Collector* onwards, he has written of strong, independent women who pose problems for the heroes. This becomes most explicit in *Mantissa* in which the 'author' comes face to face with his 'muse', who is revealed to be a rather unruly and unpredictable woman seemingly intent on disrupting his life. *A Maggot* may be seen as a historical version of the same theme: despite the novel's beginning, the heroine takes over as the object of its investigation. If this is seen as the consequence of Fowles's own attempt to come to terms with feminism, then the ideological implications should be clear. His fiction dramatizes the situation of the male striving – none too successfully – to come to terms with a redefined notion of gender.

The third theme concerns the role of the intellectual in society, and here the novel is more ambivalent in its contrast between the narrator's own sermonizing and the events of the story. Consider that the Duke's missing son is described as an intellectual, seeking esoteric knowledge. However, not only is he progressively eliminated from the novel's centre of interest, but he is also at the periphery of society, with no clear role. He is opposed to Rebecca who, far from being an intellectual, is a deeply emotional person, drawn to religion as a source of feeling and morality. Described in this way, the novel begins to look like an attempt to problematize Fowles's own situation – the impotent intellectual in a society which is decidedly anti-intellectual. His atheist's fascination with religion (one might also call it nostalgia) becomes Bartholomew's fascination with esoteric philosophy, and so the author's alienation from aspects of the dominant ideology is expressed in the novel through the character of the vanishing hero. In these three concerns, then – history, women, and the intellectual – the novel comes to express, albeit in a rather tortured way, the conflicts of a specific ideological circumstance.

It is worthwhile emphasizing at this point the precise nature of the claim being made. We are not saying that everything in the novel owes its origin to a non-individual ideological structure. Such a claim cannot account for the varieties of creative writing (even within Fowles's own output there is a great deal of variety, despite the consistencies mentioned earlier). On the other hand, we must avoid going to the opposite extreme and claiming that creative individuals can magically escape any ideological determinations through the inspiration of their own genius. Rather, we should see the novel as emerging from an ideological context (including the structures of class, gender, and nationality as existing at a particular point in history) and being mediated through the more personal factors of Fowles's psyche (derived from his own familial experience). Also making an impact on the finished product is the professional ideology of the writer (of which one aspect is the concern with the role of the intellectual). The self-consciousness apparent in both style and structure can be related to the latter – it is that which justifies the writer's status, distinguishing his work from that of other writers, both professional and non-professional.

So far we have not said much about the intended audience. Where do these ideological forces, traceable in the novel, leave the reader?

The mode of address, with its multiple positioning, avoids a strong interpellation. This is clear not just from the technique of using different voices to speak to us, but also from the very structure of the work. The device of a mystery which involves us, but which is never fully unveiled, is important here. It serves first to position us as inquirers into a specific enigma, but the novel then moves us away from this and we become witnesses of Rebecca's personal drama of feminist and religious awakening. To put it another way, the reader implied at the beginning of the novel is significantly different from the one implied by the end. Thus the single interpellated reading position of the traditional novel is avoided. The result of this is to leave the text more open and to engage the reader in a dialectic of ideological positioning. As we progress through the text we are asked to adopt a series of positions which conflict with each other. This offers to our attention an awareness of the ways in which the various 'documents' which make up the novel assume different audiences. This in turn reflects back on the reader's own ideological setting. The self-consciousness of the novel asks for an answering self-consciousness from the reader. Defamiliarization becomes not just a feature of literary technique but also an option for the reader in his or her self-awareness.

Conclusion

Thus we have a novel in which the distorted traces of ideological forces can be seen and which offers itself as an incomplete text for the reader's engagement, prompting a process of ideological self-critique if that offer is accepted in all its implications. We have reached a level of ideological complexity far beyond the simplicities of tourist brochures with which we started, and it will not be so easy to reach a clear conclusion with such a text as it was in earlier chapters (the previous chapter presented a similar case). What should be clear, however, is that at this level ideological analysis is only a partial tool. The more complex the text, the more important other complementary methods of analysis become if the work is to be fully explicated. In the case of *A Maggot*, for example, various psychoanalytic approaches would provide useful adjuncts to ideological analysis. It should also be clear that analysis of the process of reading in all its variety becomes important at this stage. But that is beyond the scope of the present book.

CONCLUSION

Our concern in this book has been to discuss and exemplify the ways in which ideology affects cultural products. In our analyses we have attempted to trace the patterning of ideological forces on texts in order to show how they mediate ideology. The inherent danger is to think that because we have performed this task, we have therefore said something important about the audience or, more generally, about the balance of political and economic power in society. The best way to counteract such a tendency is to move on from here to study the audience's reactions. As noted in chapter 2, David Morley and John Fiske have shown two very different ways in which this might be tackled. The study of ideology is an important part of the study of culture, society or the media, but is only one aspect of it. To regard it as anything more is not only reductionist but, more importantly, will inevitably lead to false conclusions about society. If the first step in changing society is understanding it, then understanding the limitations of ideological analysis is an essential part of that process.

REFERENCES

1 Defining ideology pp. 3–10
1 J. Wolff, *The Social Production of Art*, Macmillian, 1981, p. 50.
2 B. Nichols, *Ideology and the Image*, Indiana University Press, 1981, p. 1.
3 J. Fiske, *Introduction to Communication Studies*, Methuen, 1982, p. 146.
4 L. Althusser, *Essays on Ideology*, Verso, 1984, p. 45.
5 D. McLellan, *Ideology*, Open University Press, 1986, p. 1.
6 J. Larrain, *The Concept of Ideology*, Hutchinson, 1979, chapter 1.
7 J. Larrain, *Marxism and Ideology*, Macmillan, 1983, p. 54.
8 K. Marx and F. Engels, *The German Ideology, Part One*, edited with introduction by C.J. Arthur, 2nd edition, Lawrence and Wishart, 1974, p. 47.
9 ibid., p. 64.
10 T. Lovell, *Pictures of Reality*, British Film Institute, 1983, p. 51.
11 'Ideology and Ideological State Apparatuses' can be found in his *Essays on Ideology*. 'Marxism and Humanism' can be found in his *For Marx*, Verso, 1979, pp. 219–47.
12 L. Althusser, *Essays on Ideology*, p. 56.
13 L. Althusser, *For Marx*, p. 232.
14 L. Althusser, *Essays on Ideology*, pp. 67
15 Useful discussions of the base/superstructure model can be found in Raymond Williams's *Marxism and Literature*, Oxford University Press, 1977, pp. 75–82, and in Jorge Larrain's *Marxism and Ideology*, Macmillan, 1983, pp. 169–85.
16 Discussion of the concept of hegemony can be found in Robert Bocock's *Hegemony*, Tavistock, 1986, especially pp. 21–54. Extracts from Gramsci's writings on the subject can be found in *Culture, Ideology and Social Process*, edited by T. Bennett *et al.*, Batsford, 1981.

2 Processes and effects pp. 11–19
1 S. Harvey, *May '68 and Film Culture*, British Film Institute, 1978, p. 97.
2 T. O'Sullivan *et al.*, *Key Concepts in Communication*, Methuen, 1983, p. 107.
3 ibid., p. 109.
4 P. Hirst, *On Law and Ideology*, Macmillan, 1979, pp. 64–8.
5 S. Hall *et al.*, eds, *Culture, Media, Language*, Hutchinson, 1980, p. 161.
6 K. Thompson, *Beliefs and Ideology*, Tavistock, 1986, chapters 2 and 3.
7 F. Parkin, *Class Inequality and Political Order*, Paladin, 1973, pp. 81–2.
8 D. Morley, *The 'Nationwide' Audience*, British Film Institute, 1980, p. 21.

9 J. Fiske, *Understanding Popular Culture*, Unwin Hyman, 1989, pp. 20–21.
10 ibid., p. 105.
11 ibid., pp. 45–6.
12 J. Fiske, *Reading the Popular*, Unwin Hyman, 1989, chapters 4, 5a and 7.
13 E. Laclau and C. Mouffe, *Hegemony and Socialist Strategy: Toward a Radical Democratic Politics*, Verso, 1985, especially pp. 93–122.
14 ibid., p. 96.
15 J. Collins, *Uncommon Cultures: Popular Culture and Post-Modernism*, Routledge, 1989, p. 39.
16 E. Laclau and C. Mouffe, op. cit., p. 107.
17 T. Lovell, *Pictures of Reality*, British Film Institute, 1979, p. 51.
18 P. Feyerabend, *Against Method*, NLB, 1975, especially pp. 295–309.
19 D. McLellan, *Ideology*, Open University Press, 1986, p. 2.

3 Methods of analysis pp. 20–29
1 R. Williams, *Keywords*, revised edition, Fontana, 1983, pp. 87–93.
 2 ibid., p. 91.
 3 J. Fiske, *Reading the Popular*, Unwin Hyman, 1989, p. 134.
 4 R. Barthes, *Mythologies*, Paladin, 1973, pp. 109 and 129.
 5 F. Jameson, *The Political Unconscious: Narrative as a Socially Symbolic Act*, Methuen, 1981, p. 87.
 6 ibid., p. 76.
 7 ibid., pp. 87–8.
 8 ibid., p. 9.
 9 P. Macherey, *A Theory of Literary Production*, Routledge and Kegan Paul, 1978, p. 85.
10 B. Nichols, ed., *Movies and Methods*, University of California Press, 1976, pp. 493–529.
11 Judith Williamson's *Decoding Advertisements*, Marion Boyars, 1978, discusses this technique, especially on pp. 40–70.
12 Some comments on music videos along these lines can be found in E. Ann Kaplan's *Rocking Around the Clock*, Methuen, 1987, especially chapter 4 ('Ideology, adolescent desire, and the five types of video on MTV').

4 Advertising America pp. 30–38
1 The list of brochures used is as follows: Intasun, *Florida*, 2nd edition, January–November 1990; Jetsave, *America '90*, 2nd edition, 1 November 1989–31 October 1990; Jetset, *Worldwide*, November 1989–November 1990; Poundstretcher, *American Traveller*, January–October 1990; Poundstretcher, *Flights Worldwide*, November 1989–October 1990; Thomson, *Florida Fun*, 2nd edition, April–November 1990; Thomson, *Worldwide*, 2nd edition, 1 December 1989–9 December 1990; Virgin, *Virgin Territory: Florida*, December 1989–December 1990.
 2 Jetsave, op. cit., p. 62.
 3 Thomson, *Worldwide*, p. 74.
 4 Poundstretcher, *Flights Worldwide*, p. 11.
 5 Jetset, op. cit., p. 59.
 6 Virgin, op.cit., p. 12.
 7 Thomson, *Florida Fun*, p. 2.
 8 Thomson, *Worldwide*, p. 78.
 9 Virgin, op. cit., p. 88.
10 Thomson, *Worldwide*, p. 73.
11 Poundstretcher, *America Traveller*, p. 20.
12 Thomson, *Worldwide*, p. 70.
13 Intasun, op. cit., p. 70.
14 Thomson, *Florida Fun*, p. 76.
15 ibid., p. 78.

5 Opening the wall pp. 39–49

1 A good American book is *Reading the News*, edited by K. Manoff and M. Schudson, Pantheon Books, 1986. A British study of both television and newspaper news coverage is *Understanding News*, by John Hartley, Methuen, 1982, especially chapters 3, 5 and 9. Also worth consulting (although only concerned with television news) is chapter 7 of John Fiske's *Reading the Popular*, Unwin Hyman, 1989, pp. 149–84.

2 Glasgow University Media Group, *Bad News*, Routledge and Kegan Paul, 1976, and *More Bad News*, Routledge and Kegan Paul, 1980. Their later and more accessible work along the same lines can be found in *War and Peace News*, Open University Press, 1985. Criticisms of their approach can be found in *Whose News?*, by Martin Harrison, Policy Journals, 1985.

3 Daniel Hallin in K. Manoff and M. Schudson, op. cit., p. 145.

4 The most famous and influential study of news values is 'Structuring and Selecting News', by J. Galtung and M. Ruge, in *The Manufacture of News*, edited by S. Cohen and J. Young, revised edition, Constable, 1981, pp. 52–63. Hartley gives a summary and discussion of their work in *Understanding News*, chapter 5.

5 T. Henegahan, 'Just Going Over to Have a Look', *The Washington Post*, 10 November 1989, p. A39.

6 F. Protzman, 'East Berliners Explore Land Long Forbidden', *The New York Times*, 10 November 1989, p. A1.

7 K. Manoff and M. Schudson, op. cit., p. 110.

8 J. Fiske, op. cit., p. 169.

9 A. McElvoy, 'Berliners Cross the Wall to Freedom', *The Times*, 10 November 1989, p. 1.

10 F. Protzman, loc. cit.

11 P. Clough, 'East Germans Start to Travel Freely as 28-year Barrier Falls', *The Independent*, 10 November 1989, p. 1

12 R.J. McCartney, 'East Germany Opens Berlin Wall and Borders, Allowing Citizens to Travel Freely to the West', *The Washington Post*, 10 November 1989, p. A1.

13 R.D. McFadden, 'The Berlin Wall: a Monument to the Cold War, Triumphs and Tragedies', *The New York Times*, 10 November 1989, p. A15.

14 'Blast of Trumpets', *The Times*, 10 November 1989, p. 17.

15 *The Independent*, p. 8.

16 J. Fiske, op. cit., p. 178.

17 D. Hoffman and A. Devroy, 'Bush Hails "Dramatic Decision"', *The Washington Post*, 10 November 1989, p. A37.

18 *The New York Times*, p. 1.

19 *The Independent*, p. 1.

20 N. Ascherson, 'Suddenly the World Has No Edge Any More', *The Independent*, 10 November 1989, p. 1.

21 A. McElvoy, loc. cit.

22 P. Schlesinger, *Putting 'Reality' Together*, 2nd edition, Methuen, 1987, chapter 4, pp. 83–105.

6 Narrating the championship pp. 50–59

1 J. Hargreaves, *Sport, Power and Culture*, Polity Press, 1986, p. 208.

2 ibid., p. 209.

3 ibid., p. 217.

4 See for example *Sport, Culture and Ideology*, edited by J. Hargreaves, Routledge and Kegan Paul, 1982, *Sport, Culture and the Modern State*, edited by H. Cantelon and R. Gruneau, University of Toronto Press, 1982, and *Sport and Political Ideology*, by J.M. Hoberman, Heinemann, 1984.

5 N. Elias and E. Dunning, *Quest for Excitement*, Basil Blackwell, 1986, pp. 267–83.

6 T. O'Sullivan *et al.*, *Key Concepts in Communication*, Methuen, 1983, p. 149.

7 F. Jameson, *The Political Unconscious*, Methuen, 1981.

8 Ken Jones, 'Watson Waits for the Wicked Wind to Blow', *The Independent*, Thursday 20 July 1989, p. 34.

9 John Samuel, 'Seve scents the sun and dreams', *The Guardian*, Saturday 22 July 1989, p. 18.

10 Hugh McIlvanney, 'Norman's Major Mission', *The Observer*, Sunday 23 July 1989, p. 20.

11 'Golf: the Open: Harry Carpenter introduces highlights', produced by Alastair Scott and Jim Reside, BBC2, 20–23 July 1989.

12 'Golf: the Open: Introduced by Harry Carpenter', produced by Alastair Scott and Jim Reside, BBC2, 23 July 1989.

7 **Chatting to the nation** pp. 60–70

1 A good, general introduction is Mimi White's 'Ideological Analysis of Television', in *Channels of Discourse: Television and Contemporary Criticism*, edited by Robert C. Allen, Methuen, 1987, pp. 134–71. This includes a bibliography on the final four pages. John Fiske's *Television Culture*, Methuen, 1987, covers many different types of programme and frequently refers to ideology.

2 Examples include: *Coronation Street*, edited by R. Dyer *et al.*, British Film Institute, 1981; *Dr. Who: the Unfolding Text*, by J. Tulloch and M. Alvarado, Macmillan, 1983; *Everyday Television: Nationwide*, by C. Brunsdon and D. Morley, British Film Institute, 1978; *Popular Television and Film*, edited by T. Bennett *et al.*, Open University Press, 1981; and *Televising 'Terrorism'*, P. Schlesinger *et al.*, Comedia, 1983.

3 For a useful discussion of this see Jane Feuer's 'The Concept of Live Television: Ontology as Ideology', in *Regarding Television*, edited by E. Ann Kaplan, University Publications of America, 1983, pp. 12–22.

4 N. Household, 'Terry's in the Hot Seat', *Radio Times*, 16–22 February 1985, p. 8.

5 *Wogan*, directed by Tom Corcoran, produced by Jane O'Brien, executive producer Peter Estall, BBC1, 13, 15 and 17 September 1989.

6 *Broadcast*, 6 October 1989, p. 32.

7 Eartha Kitt, *I'm Still Here*, Sidgwick & Jackson, 1989; Linford Christie with Tony Ward, *Linford Christie: an Autobiography*, S. Paul, 1989; Bruce Forsyth, *Golf . . . Is It Only a Game?*, Sackville Books, 1989.

8 M. White, op. cit., p. 161.

8 **Decentred biography** pp. 71–81

1 Introductory examples include P. Biskind's *Seeing is Believing*, Pluto Press, 1984 (on Hollywood films of the fifties), and S. Heath's 'Jaws, Ideology, and Film Theory', in *Movies and Methods*, vol. 2, edited by B. Nichols, University of California Press, 1985, pp. 509–514. A more complex text is B. Nichols's *Ideology and the Image*, Indiana University Press, 1981. G. Turner analyses *Desperately Seeking Susan*, following Fiske's audience-centred approach, in *Film as Social Practice*, Routledge, 1988, pp. 167–78.

2 R.P. Kolker, *A Cinema of Loneliness*, 2nd edition, Oxford University Press, 1988, pp. 237–302.

3 ibid., p. 239.

4 *Raging Bull*, United Artists, produced by Irwin Winkler and Robert Chartoff in association with Peter Savage, directed by Martin Scorsese, script by Paul Schrader and Mardik Martin from the book *Raging Bull* by Jake La Motta with Joseph Carter and Peter Savage, leading players Robert De Niro, Cathy Moriarty, Joe Pesci, Frank Vincent and Nicholas Colasanto.

5   Martin Scorsese interviewed by David Thompson at the National Film Theatre, London, January 1987, transcribed by Jane Wollen.
6   M. Weiss, *Martin Scorsese: a Guide to References and Resources*, G.K. Hall, 1987, pp. 13–14.
7   M.P. Kelly, *Martin Scorsese: the First Decade*, Redgrave, 1980, pp. 32–4.
8   R. Combs, 'Hell Up in the Bronx', *Sight and Sound*, Spring 1981, 50/2, p. 130.
9   L. Althusser, *Essays on Ideology*, Verso, 1984, p. 174.

9   **Fictional history** pp. 82–91
1   L.J. Davis, *Resisting Novels: Ideology and Fiction*, Methuen, 1987, p. 24.
2   ibid., p. 103.
3   ibid., p. 212.
4   T. Eagleton, *Criticism and Ideology*, NLB, 1976, p. 101.
5   ibid., p. 185.
6   C. MacCabe, *Theoretical Essays: Film, Linguistics, Literature*, Manchester University Press, 1985, pp. 34–9.
7   J. Fowles, *A Maggot*, Pan Books, 1986, p. 125.
8   ibid., p. 9.
9   ibid., p. 15
10 ibid., p. 459.
11 ibid., pp. 256–67.
12 ibid., pp. 354–84.
13 ibid., pp. 359–60.
14 ibid., p. 459.
15 A. Burgess, *The Observer*, 22 September 1985, p. 27.
16 P. Rogers, *Times Literary Supplement*, 20 September 1985, p. 1027.
17 J. Fowles, op. cit., p. 442.

SELECTED ANNOTATED BIBLIOGRAPHY

ABERCROMBIE, N., HILL, S. and TURNER, B.S., *The Dominant Ideology Thesis*, Allen and Unwin, 1980.
    A detailed critique of simplistic notions of a monolithic dominant ideology, with historical evidence from feudal times to the twentieth century.

ABERCROMBIE, N., HILL, S. and TURNER, B.S., eds, *Dominant Ideologies*, Unwin Hyman, 1990.
    A collection of essays which updates the argument of the previous item by looking at the situation in a number of different countries. The chapter on 'Popular Culture and Ideological Effects' is particularly relevant to students of culture and the media.

ALTHUSSER, L., *Essays on Ideology*, Verso, 1984.
    Important for the first essay, 'Ideology and Ideological State Apparatuses', which is Althusser's most famous intervention in the ideology debate.

BARTHES, R., *Mythologies*, Jonathan Cape, 1972.
    The beginning of the ideological analysis of culture, and still an essential text. Very approachable, even if the subjects of analysis are now rather dated.

BENNETT, T. *et al.*, eds, *Culture, Ideology and Social Process*, Batsford, 1981.
    A collection of essays on culture and its relation to ideology. Particularly useful is the section of extracts from Gramsci's writings.

BERGER, J., *Ways of Seeing*, Penguin, 1972.
    A now classic study of the ways in which ideology affects our understanding of visual images, with examples ranging from Old Masters to advertisements.

BOCOCK, R., *Hegemony*, Tavistock, 1986.
    A detailed discussion of Gramsci's concept of hegemony and its relation to the work of other writers on sociology and politics.

COLLINS, J., *Uncommon Cultures: Popular Culture and Post-Modernism*, Routledge, 1989.
    A stimulating book which presents a rather different view of ideology and its relation to popular culture from the one presented in this book.

DAVIS, L.J., *Resisting Novels: Ideology and Fiction*, Methuen, 1987.
    An interesting book, even if rather too sweeping in its claims, which unravels many of the ways in which novels convey ideology, getting well beyond the simplicities of thematic approaches. Davis concentrates (although not exclusively) on the eighteenth and nineteenth-century novel.

EAGLETON, T., *Criticism and Ideology*, NLB, 1976.
    A study of ideology and literature by a well-known Marxist critic. Chapter 4 ('Ideology and Literary Form') is a particularly useful look at the ideological

position of nine major writers – Matthew Arnold, George Eliot, Charles Dickens, Thomas Hardy, Joseph Conrad, W.B. Yeats, T.S. Eliot, James Joyce and D.H. Lawrence.

EAGLETON, T., *Ideology: An Introduction*, Verso, 1991.
A clearly written, wide-ranging and energetically argued account, which takes in such writers as Schopenhauer, Freud, Habermas and Bourdieu, as well as the more obvious names. Eagleton defends a Marxist approach, arguing particularly against postmodernist writers. Unlike the previous item, this book is concerned only with theory, not with literary analysis.

FISKE, J., *Reading the Popular*, Unwin Hyman, 1989.
A companion volume to the next item, this is an interesting counterpart to ideological analysis, emphasizing the ways in which ideology is evaded and the means by which cultural texts are manipulated by the audience. It includes a wide-ranging set of analyses, with subjects ranging from shopping malls to television quiz shows.

FISKE, J., *Understanding Popular Culture*, Unwin Hyman, 1989.
Provides the theoretical justification for the analyses in the preceding text, with chapters 5 and 6 particularly relevant for questions of textual analysis.

FOWLER, R., *Language in the News: Discourse and Ideology in the Press*, Routledge, 1991.
A detailed but readable study of the use of language in British newspapers during the 1980s, which intentionally ignores all other aspects of newspaper design. Written by a professor of linguistics, it makes some use of the terminology of that discipline.

JAMESON, F., *The Political Unconscious*, Methuen, 1981.
A difficult but impressive study of ideology and literature, within a framework which can be expanded to cover cultural products in general. Not a text for beginners, but one which will continue to exert influence.

LARRAIN, J., *The Concept of Ideology*, Hutchinson, 1979.
An indispensable book which traces the development of the concept from pre-Marxists through to contemporary debates. Wide-ranging and clearly written.

LARRAIN, J., *Marxism and Ideology*, Macmillan, 1983.
A more specific and difficult text than the previous one, but it contains illuminating discussions of such issues as determination, contradiction and the base/superstructure model.

LOVELL, T., *Pictures of Reality*, B.F.I., 1983.
A discussion of Marxist theories of ideology in relation to the aesthetic debate on the nature of realism in art.

MCLELLAN, D., *Ideology*, Open University Press, 1986.
An ideal introduction to ideology, covering both Marxist and non-Marxist traditions. The emphasis is on the concept's use in political and social writing, rather than on cultural studies.

MARX, K. and ENGELS, F., *The German Ideology, Part One* (student edition), edited and introduced by C.J. Arthur, 2nd edition, Lawrence and Wishart, 1974.
There have been several editions of this classic text, but this one is the most usefully designed for students of ideology.

NICHOLS, B., *Ideology and the Image*, Indiana University Press, 1981.
A discussion of ideology and film, with the emphasis on visual style. A useful book covering documentary as well as the fiction film.

THOMPSON, J.B., *Ideology and Modern Culture*, Polity Press, 1990.
Although clearly written, Thompson develops a long and complex argument in which his intention is, as he puts it, 'to rethink ideology in the light of the development of mass communication.' His account examines the overlap of the concepts of ideology and culture and how they are related to the mass media. Not a book for beginners but one which is sure to become an important source of debate in the future.

THOMPSON, K., *Beliefs and Ideology*, Tavistock and Ellis Horwood, 1986.
A very readable introduction, much concerned with the sociology of religious belief and its link with Marxist theories of ideology. The final chapter is concerned with culture.

WILLIAMS, R., *Marxism and Literature*, Oxford University Press, 1977.
An excellent introductory, but challenging, text by one of the pioneers of cultural studies in Britain. It is concerned with a much wider area than just ideology, although this concept is central to the book. The opening chapters include a discussion of the four related concepts of culture, language, literature and ideology, and should be regarded as essential reading.

WILLIAMSON, J., *Decoding Advertisements*. Marion Boyars, 1978.
Subtitled 'ideology and meaning in advertising', this is an interesting but difficult book. Its usefulness lies in its discussion of a wide range of advertisements. Its difficulty lies in its use of a theoreteical framework derived from the psychoanalytic works of Jacques Lacan.

WOLFF, J., *The Social Production of Art*, Macmillan, 1981.
The indispensable guide to theories of art and its position within ideology. Although chapter 3 is explicitly concerned with art and ideology, the whole book is well worth reading.

INDEX